WOMEN, EDUCATION AND TRAINING

DEPARTMENT OF
PROFESSIONAL & CURRICULUM SUPPORT STUDIES

MORAY HOUSE INSTITUTE OF EDUCATION
HERIOT-WATT UNIVERSITY

WOMEN, EDUCATION AND TRAINING

Barriers to Access, Informal Starting Points and Progression Routes

Veronica McGivney

**DEPARTMENT OF
PROFESSIONAL & CURRICULUM SUPPORT STUDIES**

**MORAY HOUSE INSTITUTE OF EDUCATION
HERIOT-WATT UNIVERSITY**

HILLCROFT COLLEGE
NIACE

Published by the National Institute of Adult Continuing
Education and Hillcroft College, 1993

Reprinted 1994

British Library Cataloguing in Publication Data
A CIP record for this book is available from the British Library

ISBN 1 872941 42 7

*The views expressed are those of the author and do not
necessarily reflect those of the government department which
funded the study or of Hillcroft College or NIACE.*

Cover photo courtesy Leicestershire Community Education

*Printed and bound in Great Britain by
Biddles Ltd, Guildford and King's Lynn*

CONTENTS

DEPARTMENT OF
PROFESSIONAL & CURRICULUM SUPPORT STUDIES

MORAY HOUSE INSTITUTE OF EDUCATION
HERIOT-WATT UNIVERSITY

ACKNOWLEDGEMENTS

During the project, visits were made to:

- WEA West Lancashire and Cheshire District Office
- Asian women tutors at Preston WEA area office
- The Women's Technology Scheme, Liverpool
- The tutor of the Women's Issues course, Liverpool
- Rotunda Community College, Vauxhall
- Parents in Education course, Broadgreen Infants School, Liverpool
- The LiverBus
- East Leeds Women's Workshop
- Castleford Women's Centre and one of its outlying centres
- Women in Focus Consultancy and the Wider Horizons Day, Newcastle
- Swindon WEA Women's Branch
- The tutor of New Opportunities for Black Women courses, Thameside
- Working with People course, Goldsmiths' College.

Many thanks are due to all the people who organised the visits and gave up their time to discuss their work with me, and to those who assisted the project by sending information or materials, discussing their work over the telephone or suggesting contacts: Eileen Aird, Niormal Arya and Fauzia Ullah, Chris Atkinson and Carol Gorman, Brigid Baillie, Beryl Bateson, Jan Campbell, Barbara Blanche, Marie McGivern and other staff on the LiverBus, Dorothy Clarke, Maggie Coats, Pam Cole, Joyce Deere, Julita Edwards, Dorothea Hall, Cathy Hull, Ruth Howlett, Brenda James, Bev, Marilyn and Jane at East Leeds Women's Workshop, Dianne Jenkins, Graham Jones, Dania Leslie, Gill Moglione, Tricia McCredie, Libby McKay and women students at Rotunda Community College, Joanna McMinn, Jackie Morgan, Maureen Patterson, Katherine Quigley, Jill Stevens and women students at the Parents in Education course, Broadgreen Infants School, Cathy Shea, Barbara Smith, Jane Straw, Kathy Tiernan, Tricia Wargent, Judy Woodman, B.H. Yemm, Paula Ziane, Mavis Zutshi.

Thanks are also due to members of the project Steering Committee for their advice and support – Eileen Aird, Maggie Coats, Joyce Deere, Julita Edwards, Roy Grey, Pauline Sagoe-Staff and Alastair Thomson.

INTRODUCTION

This study, funded by the Employment Department Training, Enterprise and Education Directorate, was conducted in an 80-day period during 1992–3 by Dr Veronica McGivney, Research and Development Officer of the National Institute of Adult Continuing Education. It was managed and administered by Hillcroft Women's College.

Aims and Objectives

The general aims of the study were to refine definitions of women's education and training needs and to identify the factors that assist or impede their access, participation and progression within education and training. The objectives were:

- to identify and analyse the barriers that inhibit many women from moving directly into mainstream formal education and training
- to explore the role of informal, community-based re-entry schemes in increasing women's confidence and motivation to learn
- to identify the factors which account for the effectiveness of such schemes in helping women to progress in various ways
- to examine and analyse the various transferable features and components of identified learning schemes and identify the common processes involved in helping women to regain the confidence to move to other levels of education
- to analyse the experience and perceptions of participants who have moved into other forms and levels of education and training
- to define key issues relating to transition, progression and student support
- to produce a report and briefing paper to assist policy-makers and education and training providers in providing effective education/training routes for women.

Methods

The project employed a two-pronged approach:

1. A literature search: a wide range of sociological and educational research reports, books, articles, project and course reports were consulted.

2. Contact, through correspondence, telephone and visits, with people working in education and training courses and projects which have an established record in encouraging women to progress to further education, training or employment. During visits, interviews were conducted with staff and some students.

The names of the projects, centres and courses visited and all the people who contributed to the project are listed in the Acknowledgements.

The Conduct of the Project

During the visits made for the project, it was found that the obstacles to access and participation mentioned by tutors and students were largely the same as those frequently cited in the literature of access. It seemed more useful, therefore, to concentrate in the interviews on those aspects of women's courses and schemes which encourage and help women to progress to further education, training and employment.

The Report

Several difficulties emerged during the writing of this report. Firstly, the problem of how to deal with women without adopting a deficit approach. Although there is no denying that many women experience difficulty in gaining access to and participating in appropriate education or training, it must be stated clearly from the outset that women themselves are not the problem. The problems reside in a number of interrelated factors: socially transmitted attitudes and expectations; domestic constraints; stereotyping in training and the labour market; policies and institutions that are unresponsive to women's life patterns and needs.

Secondly, although women cannot be considered as one huge and undifferentiated group, it was difficult to deal with different groups of women separately without being overlengthy and repetitious. It was decided, therefore, to refer to specific groups of women when particularly relevant, for example in relation to the differential impact of various factors on their ability to participate.

A third problem was how to produce a useful publication which is not just another 'recipe book' itemising barriers and needs which have already been frequently identified. This was a difficult problem to avoid since it is impossible to write a report on women, education and training without reference to the multiple obstacles to access and participation that women continue to face and which need to be removed if gender equality in education, training and the labour market is to be achieved. The fact that women still cite the same obstacles after a decade of attention to access issues renders their repetition essential, especially now that the restructuring of adult education and training is bringing new people into the field who may not be instinctively responsive to women's needs or familiar with the existing literature of access.

Nevertheless, this report seeks to be more than just a recipe book by attempting to place the barriers women experience in a wider social and cultural context, and by examining the importance of providing not only accessible starting points for women learners but also measures which actively encourage and facilitate their progression to formal education and training.

The Format of the Report

The report is in five sections:

- Section 1 analyses the reasons for conducting the project.
- Section 2 examines the obstacles that prevent many women from undertaking a formal education or training course.
- Section 3 identifies the features and components of introductory or re-entry courses that are effective in giving women the confidence and motivation to progress to further education or training.
- Section 4 considers the factors that help or hinder women's transition from informal introductory learning programmes to formal education, training and employment.
- Section 5 considers the findings of the project in the light of recent developments and trends in education and training for adults.

- An Appendix outlines some courses and initiatives which have been effective in helping women's access and progression.

SECTION 1

The Need for Improved Access and Progression Routes

Continuing Inequalities

There have been repeated calls over the last decade for more and better quality education and training opportunities for women; for greater flexibility of access and delivery and for greater practical support for women in education and training. In response, there have been positive developments in some areas: many education providers now take women's practical constraints into consideration in the timetabling and organisation of some courses; more educational institutions now have some, albeit limited, childcare facilities; and there has been steady growth in some curriculum areas, such as targeted Access courses and courses for women 'returners'.

Unfortunately, such developments have not had any discernible impact on the position of women in the British labour market. Despite the sex discrimination legislation of the 1970s, wide social and economic changes, and the fact that increasing numbers of women have been entering paid employment, women are still far from achieving equality in the labour market and women over 25 are the least qualified segment of the working population:

- 52 per cent of British women are in or seeking paid employment
- 5 million are in part-time employment (Britain has the highest number of part-time workers in the EC)
- British women earn less as a percentage of men's pay than women in any other EC country (55 per cent in the case of full-time white collar workers, 69 per cent in the case of manual workers) (Equal Opportunities Commission, 1992).

'We do not need lengthy pieces of research to tell us that working women are concentrated in low paid, low skilled and low status jobs. We can see that for ourselves' (East Leeds Women's Workshop, 1991, 3).

1

A number of disadvantages flow from women's position in the labour market:

- women are more vulnerable than men to economic change because they are concentrated in a much narrower range of occupations and industries
- the majority of women's part-time jobs are low paid and insecure and carry no pension rights, sickness benefits, developmental training or promotion prospects
- there are fewer structured training opportunities in traditional female occupations than in male-dominated areas.

Forecasts that women will be recruited to the labour market to compensate for labour and skills shortages are now beginning to sound increasingly hollow. Although there has been growth in low paid, part-time jobs for women, there are few signs of real improvement in their employment prospects at a time of rapidly growing unemployment. There is also little evidence that employers have started to give priority to the recruitment or retention of women workers. A survey conducted by Hampshire TEC, for example, found that only 18 per cent of local employers planned to recruit women, and that the majority were aiming to recruit experienced staff and school-leavers (Women Returners' Network, 1991).

Dwindling Education and Training Opportunities

Demand from women for education and training has spread to all sectors. Women have been entering further and higher education in increasing numbers for over a decade, and their take-up of general adult education opportunities invariably exceeds that of men. Women's demand for work-related training has also increased. A survey in Northern Ireland found that 96 per cent of women between the ages of 25 and 50 wanted basic education, training or retraining (McCorry, 1988). Over 60 per cent of the 57,000 calls received by a BBC Helpline on education, training, enterprise and careers during one week in 1992 were from women (Educational Broacasting for the UK, 1992).

However, the demand for training, particularly from women in their thirties and forties, is not always matched by supply, and, in general, fewer women than men gain access to work-related training schemes. Payne (1991) argues that the thrust of current training policy has resulted in a reduction in training opportunities for women: the gradual shifting of training costs to employers and trainees discriminates against women, who traditionally receive less training from employers and, because of lower pay, are less able to invest in their own training. Payne also points out that the narrow eligibility criteria governing national training programmes, together with the policy not to provide childcare, results in the exclusion of many unwaged and unemployed women. A report by the Women's National Commission (1992) also expresses reservations about national training schemes. It argues that financial pressures on the Training and Enterprise Councils (TECs) have reduced women's prospects of receiving good quality training and that despite examples of excellent practice, some TECs do not appear to be making proper assessments of the needs of potential women returners when drawing up their business plans.

Within other sectors opportunities for women also appear to be dwindling. In adult and community education, a sector in which women traditionally comprise the majority of learners, public expenditure cuts and structural changes are taking their toll. The removal, under the 1992 Further and Higher Education Act, of specified (Schedule 2) courses to the centrally-funded further education sector is likely to have a significant impact on adult education structures, syllabuses, fees and the status of remaining programmes. The consequences are already apparent in some areas. According to research conducted by the National Institute of Adult Continuing Education, some Local Education Authorities have been obliged to reduce or cut their adult provision or run it on a full cost recovery basis, to change the balance of the courses offered, to increase fees and reduce fee concessions (Powell and Winkless, 1992; Winkless, 1993). Another predicted consequence of the Act is that the number of local access points for adult learning will be sharply reduced. As many working with adults have pointed out, women, as the majority of learners, will be most affected by these changes:

> Just when the needs of women seemed to be recognised; when many of the arguments seemed to have been won, we are faced with the need not just to build for the future but to battle for our survival (Coats, 1992a).

Diminishing Concern with Equal Opportunities

The Further and Higher Education Act prioritises vocational, certificated and Access programmes for adults. Such provision is aimed at people who have defined specific educational or vocational objectives and who are motivated, ready and able to participate. A much larger number of individuals are not in this position. These are often people – many of them women – whose attitudes and aspirations have been shaped by negative school experiences and cultural assumptions based on class, race or gender, and whose domestic and material situation and level of educational 'preparedness' preclude the possibility of entering formal education or training. Recent policy shifts and changes in adult and further education have contributed to a gradual erosion of informal and targeted local initiatives which aim to increase the participation of the groups most under-represented in education and training, a trend exacerbated by the cutting back or elimination of programmes enabling work with special groups, for example the REPLAN Programme and the Urban Programme. These developments, combined with the economic situation and the growth in unemployment, appear to be having an impact on the profile of adult learners. A pilot survey in one university adult and continuing education department showed that the shift from non-certificated and general interest programmes towards training and PICKUP courses has inevitably brought in a different clientele, consisting largely of urban business and professional groups and mature students seeking entry to degree courses (Hester and Florence, 1992).

Changes have also been observed in the clientele of general education classes. A survey of local authorities (Powell and Winkless, 1992) suggests that younger married men and women, often unemployed and seeking to re-enter the labour market, are now turning to adult education to obtain qualifications and skills. This trend is reflected in the results of a survey of foreign language courses (Centre for Information on Language Teaching and Research, 1992), in which 45 per cent of responding adult education centres reported a significant change in the composition of students, with more men, more younger learners and more people joining for work-related reasons. This is a welcome trend, but it is worrying that at the same time opportunities appear to be dwindling for the large numbers of people who require help at an earlier stage, in the form of introductory and exploratory re-entry programmes to start them on the route back into education and training. Overall, however, there appears to be a gradual shift away from the sort of curriculum which starts 'where the student is', characteristic of education with women and a number of under-represented groups during the 1980s, towards a curriculum starting 'where the market is'. The decision to focus in this project on the re-entry or 'threshold' stage was taken because of signs of a diminishing concern for women who have no or limited access to formal education and training.

There is, nevertheless, a widespread belief, contradicted by the evidence, that women have achieved equality of opportunity in education and training and that no further measures to accommodate their needs are necessary. During this project, a number of contacts and interviewees reported that educational institutions and TECs were discontinuing, or putting a ceiling on, initiatives aimed at women, on the grounds that everything necessary had already been done or that 'saturation point' had been reached. In nearly all cases, this complacency was based on there having been an equal opportunities policy and one or two special courses or activities for women during the last few years.

In further and higher education, the argument that equality has been achieved is invariably based on the fact that the numbers of women students have steadily increased over the last decade. By 1990 women comprised 49 per cent of all mature full-time students and 45 per cent of mature part-time students in higher education (DFE Statistical Bulletin, 18/92). The overall numerical increase, however, masks the fact that there has been little adjustment of the gender balance throughout institutions. Women staff are still extremely under-represented in senior management posts in both higher and further education, while students are still over-concentrated in a limited number of subject areas. It has been observed that an apparently dramatic increase in the number of women students in an institution may be entirely due to the existence of one or two targeted Access or updating courses:

> The concentration of women in certain types of provision can make it seem that their position is more secure than it actually is: the cessation of that course would occasion a drastic reduction. It also means that women who do not see that course as the best for them are NOT being provided for, and it shows that what is taken to be 'overall' provision is, in fact, predominantly men's provision answering the requirements of very few women (Hester and Florence, 1992: 49–50).

Programmes provided specifically for women tend to be designated as 'special' provision, i.e. programmes which deviate from the mainstream norm. There are dangers in perceiving education for women mainly in terms of 'special' targeted courses or projects. However, women are likely to continue to demand targeted programmes so long as formal education and training remain permeated by a male culture, with women's education and training needs viewed as deviant and problematic rather than simply different. Women are expected to 'fit in' with existing education and training provision. There has been no comprehensive attempt to adapt further and higher education and training to women's requirements, which are little understood or analysed, and little attempt to analyse their position and experience in relation to the whole field of education and training, including adult and community education, where women students predominate.

Under-Reporting of Women in Education and Training

Although there is a body of knowledge relating to the courses such as New Opportunities for Women undertaken during the 1980s, women's education and their experience in education remain largely uncharted. A decade ago, Thompson (1983) observed that adult and community education tutors failed to attach any particular significance to the fact that they were working mainly with women, and the organisation and delivery of courses took little account of the social, economic, cultural and political conditions of being female in this society. A similar point was made by Bruce (1984), who observed that studies of community education in Scotland were characterised by the 'invisibility' of women as a concern, even though they composed the majority of students. Referring to a then recently published work on informal learning networks, she noted that only 12 of 250 pages were primarily concerned with women learners.

A decade on there is little evidence of change. Hester and Florence (1992) have found that very little 'broad-sweep' research within adult education is 'gender-aware on a deep level', and a recent analysis of British and American adult education journals has revealed that gender is rarely considered as significant, although up to two-thirds or more of the subjects of the studies and articles are women: 'Many of the research findings were primarily based on women, yet authors rarely recognized this fact or considered its impact on the results' (Hayes, 1992: 136).

One may hazard guesses as to the reasons for this omission. It could, as Hester and Florence (1992) suggest, reflect an 'outmoded universalising approach in which human subjectivity is unified and unproblematic, with social groups commonsensically supposed to have broadly compatible aims and aspirations'. This fits with the long-established tendency to explain educational underprivilege mainly in social class terms. Alternatively, it could stem from a deep-seated resistance to opening up the issue of gender and education because of the striking social and economic inequalities that the process would inevitably reveal.

It is worth mentioning in passing, however, that the dearth of gender-based information and analysis is not confined to education. It is rare for data collection processes to take gender into account even in areas where there are obvious and striking differences between the sexes. For example, a group collecting information about older women for the Women's National Commission have found it very difficult to obtain gender-related information, although older women greatly outnumber older men in the population (mentioned at the aunch of WNC report on older women, London, 1 December 1992).

Even those most actively involved in women's education have sometimes failed to analyse and evaluate their work and its significance. The development of women's education, interpreted here widely as courses specifically designed for women and focused on their interests, life-styles and learning needs, has been characterised, according to one critique, by 'a multitude of piecemeal, haphazard and pragmatic approaches':

> *Information about courses has not been widely disseminated, with the consequence that the lessons from experience are not available in any usable form. Although information is often gathered from individual courses and is sometimes published, accounts of this kind tend to rely heavily on anonymous quotations from delighted students and descriptions of course organisation and content; are almost invariably concerned with a small number of students, rarely follow them up beyond the first port of call after the courses and do not usually attempt to locate the work within any kind of theoretical context (Malcolm, 1992: 53–54).*

Leaving aside the fact that few if any post-school providers track the destinations of their students beyond the first port of call, this indictment ignores the fact that women's education has deliberately sought to change not only adult education but also research methodologies, by eschewing an academic approach and involving students themselves; it also ignores the fact that many courses and schemes designed for women have been conducted on a shoestring, outside the further and higher education sectors, by part-time tutors with little time to spare to analyse and theorise their work. The funding of such courses rarely if ever includes resources to conduct a systematic and long-term assessment of outcomes and progression. A WEA women's tutor interviewed for this project referred to the difficulty of conducting thorough evaluations while funded on a stop-go, short-term basis: 'We're really hampered by not being able to demonstrate systematically what we do'.

Informal schemes such as those outlined in Section 3, which have been demonstrably successful in helping women without qualifications to discover an enthusiasm for learning and establish the confidence and motivation to seek further education and training, are usually characterised by limited staff and resources and acute financial insecurity. There is an urgent and continuing need for such projects, since many women still experience a great number of obstacles which prevent them from participating in formal education and training. The finding of a national survey (Woodley *et al.*, 1987) that working-class women were 'massively' under-represented in all forms and levels of post-school education is probably equally true today. Other groups, such as minority ethnic women and those with disabilities, also face considerable barriers. So, it could be argued, do similar groups of men. However, women encounter a wider and more complex range of constraints, although their impact varies according to other factors which interact with gender to shape women's experience and the way they are perceived and treated in society.

At a time when the context of adult learning is rapidly changing and national education and training targets have been established to create a more educated, qualified and flexible workforce, a re-examination of the conditions that assist or block women's routes into and through education and training seems timely.

Summary Points

- Women face continuing inequalities in the labour market. Education and training opportunities for women are dwindling.
- There are signs of a diminishing concern with equal opportunities.
- Women's position and experiences in education and training have been under-analysed and under-reported.
- The establishment of national education and training targets means that greater attention should be paid to the factors which help or hinder women's access, participation and progression.

SECTION 2

Barriers to Access and Participation

We cannot speak about education and training opportunities for women as though all women were the same. Variables such as age, social class, race, educational background and attainment, economic circumstances, health, disability, marital status and sexuality create huge differences between women. Different groups – women with disabilities, black women, women from non-English-speaking backgrounds, single parents, rural and isolated women – inevitably experience problems and constraints in relation to education or training that are specific to their respective situations. At some of the projects visited in the course of this research there were also significant differences, in terms of attitudes, concerns, aspirations and needs, between women with pre-school or school-aged children and women whose children were no longer so dependent on them.

There is no attempt here, therefore, to present a white middle-class woman's experience as universally valid. Just as, in the past, gender issues have tended to get lost in an all-embracing concern with social class, so there is a danger that race issues become subsumed within an all-embracing concern with gender. Too exclusive a focus on gender may lead to feelings of exclusion and irrelevance among black women.

To acknowledge difference, however, is not to deny that there are commonalities based on gender. Many women seeking education, training or employment come up against certain barriers whatever their race or class. At a black women's project the co-ordinators stressed that although black women have specific problems in relation to the wider community, when they seek to participate in education and training they experience many of the same obstacles as white women. These obstacles require restating: firstly, because they are still not adequately recognised or addressed in education and training policy; secondly, because education and training opportunities for adults in Britain are undergoing a process of rapid structural change which means that providers and individuals who have not hitherto worked in this field may now be required to respond to the education and training needs of women.

Some Common Obstacles

During the project reported here, the researcher attended a TEC-funded Wider Horizons event for women in Tyneside. This attracted 30 women aged between 20 and 55: a group with wide differences in social class, personal circumstances, educational background and attainment (some women had few or no qualifications, some had degrees) and occupational background (some had never been in paid employment, some had previously held high status jobs). Despite such differences, it was striking that the difficulties participants identified in relation to gaining access to education, training and employment were broadly similar. They fell into three broad clusters:

Personal and domestic constraints

- lack of qualifications and work experience
- negative school experiences
- lack of childcare
- lack of support from male partners and families
- pressure or discouragement from others
- lack of money for education/training.

Dispositional or psychological constraints

- lack of confidence, drive or motivation
- fear (of not being clever enough)
- lack of a clearly identified direction
- the 'guilt factor' (*vis-à-vis* domestic/family responsibilities).

Structural constraints

- lack of jobs
- lack of training schemes
- lack of information on the opportunities available
- lack of guidance.

The problems identified by the women in Tyneside correspond broadly with those which have been frequently identified in surveys and course reports from all over the country. If we examine them in more detail, the extent to which the obstacles to women's participation are inter-related and mutually reinforcing becomes clear.

Practical and Material Constraints

It is well established that women's ability to participate in education, training and paid employment is hugely affected by their family structure, domestic commitments and economic circumstances. On a wider level it is affected by labour market conditions and occupational structures.

Domestic commitments and the 'career break'

Women who take a break from paid work in order to care for their children rarely return to work at the same level, even if they have good qualifications. The longer the break, the greater the likelihood that they will not be able to catch up on the lost years. This process of downward mobility has been traced by Payne:

> When they go back to work, a large proportion move one or more rungs down the occupational ladder to less skilled and less responsible jobs. They are particularly likely to experience downward mobility if they have been away from work for a number of years and if – as most do – they go back to work part-time. When women do get good qualifications, the jobs they get are often well below the jobs their education has fitted them for (Payne, 1991: 8–9).

Thus women are at a severe disadvantage in the labour market: two factors in particular – women's traditional family role and occupational sex stereotyping – work together in trapping them in employment with low pay and limited prospects:

> Working at a low skill level makes the problem of decaying skills and confidence even worse, and low wages mean that women cannot afford childcare and the other facilities they need if they are to give more of their time to paid employment. From the employers' point of view, such women are a cheap and dispensable workforce in which they are unlikely to invest (Payne, 1991: 145–6).

One way to combat this situation would be for women to obtain appropriate training or retraining. Here, however, a vicious circle is in evidence. Women's ability to participate in education and training is hampered by exactly the same factors that contribute to their disadvantaged position in the labour market.

11

Lack of childcare and eldercare facilities

It is universally accepted, at least by women, that the facility that would most assist women's return to education or training would be local day care services to support them in their role as carers not just of children but, increasingly, of older, sick and disabled relatives. It is one of the contradictions in society's attitudes to women, however, that although the virtues of caring for children, elderly and sick family members are extolled, there is very little support for the women fulfilling these roles. Britain's poor record on public provision for pre-school children is well known and there is even less support for women who care for dependent adults.

The impact this has on women's education, training and employment prospects should not be under-estimated. A survey of 750 women in Glamorgan and Gwent revealed that 88 per cent of those not currently training would enter training if childcare were available and 78 per cent of those participating in training courses would return to work full-time if suitable childcare were available (Chwarae Teg, 1992). The dearth of good and affordable publicly-provided childcare is one of the most commonly cited practical obstacles to women's participation in education and training in Britain.

Lack of finance

The next most frequently cited barrier is the cost of entering education and training. Payne's (1991) analysis of women's participation in the former Training Opportunities Scheme (TOPs) revealed that a considerable number of women trainees had wanted to undertake education or training at an earlier date but had not succeeded in doing so because of family commitments and financial constraints. This picture is confirmed by countless other surveys indicating that women who want to train or retrain are predominantly deterred by lack of personal finance for fees, childcare and travel. A regional survey in the Norfolk and Waveney area revealed the tremendous financial barriers experienced by people, particularly women, seeking vocational training (DeBell and Davies, 1991). DeBell (1992) has itemised the potential 'cluster of costs' faced by individuals undertaking work-related training without financial assistance from employers or central and local government:

- training and course fees
- add-on costs (books, equipment, examination fees, registration fees)
- direct personal and family support costs while training
- childcare costs (if provision available)

- dependent relative care costs (if provision available)
- transport costs (depending on availability, frequency and reliability of provision)
- location, timing and duration of training where it incurs additional costs
- costs of physical access, training support and technical support aids for people with special training needs.

The research in East Anglia found that many adults were obliged to drop out of training for financial reasons, sometimes because of inability to pay the examination fees. DeBell (1992) argues that the costs of long, certificated training courses have obliged many adults to confine themselves to successive short courses which do not lead to certification and which may fail to meet their aspirations and potential. However, many women may also be deterred by the costs of short training courses, particularly if full fee payment is demanded in advance. Moreover, it has been found that women with families are often reluctant to spend family money on their own needs and they may not be able to obtain financial assistance for a number of reasons: part-time education and training does not qualify for grant support in most LEAs and the practice of part or full fee remission varies widely between authorities, as does provision of discretionary grants. Currently, there are signs that both of these mechanisms for student support are dwindling as a result of public spending cuts and structural changes.

Women tend to be both disqualified from full fee remission and to be reluctant to use money for their own training needs. They are, in many cases, additionally excluded from part fee remission. Again and again the research team found that women placed family and children above their own training needs in managing household budgets (DeBell, 1992: 9).

If a women does receive financial help towards the costs of education or training, this may be deducted from any welfare benefits her husband may receive. If she obtains assistance towards full-time attendance, this may lead to loss of any Income Support or Unemployment Benefit she may receive.

The profoundly negative impact of these two factors – lack of good, affordable childcare and education and training costs – on women's ability to enter education, training and paid employment has been afforded scant attention in social, economic, education or training policies.

Lack of transport

Women in rural and suburban areas are often physically isolated.

13

Women have less access to private vehicles than men and fewer of them drive. Inadequate or expensive public transport can be an additional barrier to those who need to travel a long distance to the nearest centre providing education and training opportunities. This particularly affects women in outlying estates and rural areas poorly provided with services and facilities. It has been found that even a distance of three miles between villages will prevent people without transport from attending classes (Further Education Unit, undated). In addition, many women have fears about their personal safety and do not like travelling at night.

Issues of timing

The timing of available courses is therefore another important issue. Women with school-aged children may be able to attend courses for certain hours during the day but their ability to attend courses at other times or on a full-time basis is severely constrained.

Research and course reports over the last decade have consistently provided evidence of these practical barriers. As they are the most frequently cited obstacles to women's participation in education and training, it is all too easy, as Cole (1988) suggests, to believe that provision of a few targeted, low-cost and geographically accessible courses with some childcare facilities is all that is needed to give women equal access to education and training. However, token action of this kind can be counterproductive to women's interests. As Malcolm (1992) argues, it simultaneously keeps women's education separate and distinct from the mainstream and provides a convenient excuse for not examining the whole of institutional provision in relation to women students. Like some medical remedies, the provision of a few 'special' courses for women addresses the symptoms rather than the cause. The practical constraints that limit women's choices and ability to participate in education, employment and many areas of public life are merely the observable effects of the cultural expectations of and attitudes towards women that are so much part of the fabric and mores of society that they are scarcely acknowledged, let alone subjected to widespread challenge.

Cultural Constraints

In this society as in many others, economic and power structures, from the centre down to individual organisations, are massively male-dominated, as evidenced by:

- legislation, social policy and institutional structures which reflect male career patterns and concerns
- lack of women in policy-making positions
- limited opportunities in employment and public life available to women
- persistent gender stereotyping in the labour market.

In her review of research into the psychological and sociological factors that constrain women's freedom and choices, Deere (1988) cites some of the cultural processes which affect women's opportunities but which do not apply to men, namely:

- sex-role socialisation
- sex discrimination
- marital/familial status
- role (home–career) conflict
- occupational stereotyping.

While all of these processes affect all women to some degree, the extent of their impact varies according to individual circumstances and factors such as race and social class which interact with gender to create a whole structure of under-privilege: 'Racism, sexism and "classism" have become systematised into a philosophy of race, gender and class superiority which is central to the way our society is organised as a whole' (Arshad, 1992).

Sex-role socialisation

Sex-role socialisation starts virtually at birth. Girls quickly assimilate what is expected of them in terms of appropriate behaviour in order to gain acceptance and approval. According to March (1991), concepts of gender roles, desirable behaviours and appropriate expectations are learnt from a very early age. Deere (1988) cites British research showing how the process of sex-role socialisation is already observable by the time children reach primary school. Children quickly learn, for example, that certain attributes are perceived as 'male' – competitiveness, assertiveness, self-directedness, independence, achievement-orientation. Girls, on the other hand, are expected to be person-centred, passive and lacking in personal ambition. These stereotyped expectations and assumptions have a powerful impact on girls, militating against their participation in activities and interests perceived as being for males, and often stunting their academic and career prospects. Bateson (1991) cites research on female attitudes to achievement which indicates that many girls fear success in a mixed competitive setting as it might result in 'loss of femininity and social rejection'.

15

The assumption that girls are destined mainly to be wives and mothers operates not only as a brake on their own ambitions but also affects the judgement of many of those in a position to advise, guide and employ them. Deere (1988), for example, cites research indicating that fewer girls are sent on day release schemes because of a perception that their commitment to work will be short-term.

Constraints on behaviour and mobility

In some respects, attitudes to women can be seen to be stuck in a time-warp, resisting the enormous social and economic changes wrought this century by international events, wars, altered demographic patterns, the introduction of the welfare state and social and educational legislation. They reflect a persisting but unacknowledged cultural drive to restrict women as far as possible to the private and domestic domain. The continuing low level of representation of women in political and public life and in the upper managerial echelons of most occupations and professions is a situation easily and frequently deplored but readily sustained through social and employment policies.

Discussing the processes that create and maintain women's inequality in society, Walters (1992) points out that relationships between men and women are not randomly structured but are underpinned by economic and political arrangements, of which ideological structures are part. She cites a study which identifies the two main mechanisms of patriarchy as sexual division of labour, which allocates men and women to different occupations and consequently to differential levels of prestige and reward, and control of women's sexuality, which constrains women's space and physical mobility and shapes conceptions of what women should be. For example, concepts such as virginity, honour and safety act both as constraints on women's behaviour and as justifications for denying them certain rights (although not all men and women use or respond to male power in the same way). According to the study cited by Walters, the two mechanisms 'function in a mutually supportive manner, one justifying the other, making the combination seem totally natural and rendering the questioning of either of them a formidable task, since economic benefits and deeply internalised norms of reality are then at stake' (Walters, 1992: 1–2).

As a result of cultural perceptions of what are appropriate activities and arenas for them, women, depending on social class, age, ethnicity, etc., experience varying degrees of constraint on their freedom of movement. Deem (1992) argues that cultural views of the activities which women should engage in affect all women and ac-

16

count for the fact that there are relatively few places where women can meet socially with other women in a non-threatening atmosphere. She cites studies on the extent to which women in public places in British society are expected to behave in circumscribed ways and how men 'police' public and social meeting places to ensure that women are either made to feel uncomfortable or keep away altogether. In one of the urban areas visited during this project, education workers on the LiverBus referred to powerful cultural restrictions on working-class women's choices and activities: 'This is a very conservative and traditional area. Everything works through family links. The structures are largely male-dominated and women don't seem to come out from under. There aren't any structures here for them.'

Unequal power within relationships

Many women who stay at home to care for families experience restrictions on their social and spatial autonomy. Unless they can afford domestic help or childcare, economic dependency combines with cultural attitudes and expectations to create a situation of inequality, although the extent to which this is experienced inevitably varies according to individuals and individual circumstances:

> Research on decision-making within families in western societies has demonstrated that the balance of power usually resides with the husband. ... The ability to maintain authority and influence others within marriage depends on the resources which each partner brings to the relationship ... factors such as education, income and occupational status will increase a partner's autonomy and provide him or her with more leverage when engaging in effective decision-making. In most cases, of course, married women will have fewer resources in this sense than their husbands (Stott and Pill, 1990: 61).

Unequal power relations within the family are frequently exposed when mothers seek to participate in any activity, interest or employment outside the home which is not related to their domestic role and which entails some change to the domestic routine. At this point, some women experience resistance from male partners and other family members. Many consequently abandon their outside interests for the sake of family peace and comfort. Research into the leisure activities of women with pre-school children (Wimbush, 1988) revealed that mothers of young children, unlike their male partners, seldom considered that they had a right to personal leisure. They were more often 'the servicers, providers and spectators of the leisure of others within the family than participants in activities responding to their own interests, preferences or needs'. Where there were conflicts between the demands or needs of family members and the mothers' outside commitments, it was generally the women's leisure that was cut back or dropped. The obstacles to participation in outside activities most frequently cited by respondents to this survey are identical to those frequently reported in educational research: lack of support with childcare, shortage of personal time and money and lack of drive and self-motivation. Wimbush contends that these constraints operate through a powerful combination of cultural processes:

- the ideological construction of motherhood symbolised by self-denial (the good mother devotes all her time, energy and resources to the needs of the family)
- sexual division of labour where caring roles are defined as family obligations for which women are held responsible
- the unpaid status of housework and the lack of clearly-defined standards and working hours
- the low social priority attached to the social needs of children and their carers in the provision of public amenities, facilities and services.

Wimbush's study reveals the extent to which male partners play a 'gate-keeping' role in either facilitating or constraining a woman's participation in activities outside the home. Even those who initially encouraged their wives' activities withdrew co-operation and support in proportion to the greater demands made upon their time. Significantly, the Wimbush study found a striking difference between respondents in one- and two-parent households, with single mothers expressing a greater sense of personal independence and social and financial autonomy despite their more restricted budgets and resources.

Another study (Stott and Pill, 1990) provides further evidence of unequal power relations within families and the power of male partners to block women's desired courses of action. This study into ways of changing family diet patterns revealed that women tend to subordinate their own food preferences to those of their partners and that, contrary to general belief, they do not exert a decisive influence on family eating habits. In fact, any attempts by women who took part in the study to initiate changes for themselves or for the family as a whole were often thwarted through lack of support from husbands and, to a lesser extent, children. Like Wimbush's research, this study found that women were more likely to accommodate their husbands' wishes and changes in behaviour than vice versa, and that any alteration to their own behaviour pattern was only likely to succeed in so far as the

change was acceptable to the rest of the family and did not affect their
routine or life-style to any great degree.

Stott and Pill's review of research suggests that the pattern of
influence within families varies according to the respective subcul-
tures to which they belong. They cite studies which have found that
less educated and lower-paid husbands exert the most power within
families. This has also been found in research into educational non-
participation. Some surveys have identified married women in lower
income groups in deprived working-class areas as one of the groups
most lacking in personal autonomy and with least control over their
own lives (Hedoux, 1981; McGivney, 1990a).

Unequal power relationships within male–female partnerships
therefore have a strong bearing on women's ability to engage in
education or training.

Opposition to women's participation in education and training

In Britain, many tutors working with women have found that male
opposition to their partner's participation is commonplace. It is a
phenomenon which affects women in all social classes. In an interview
conducted for this project, the tutor of a training scheme for black
women identified the two main obstacles they face as lack of childcare
and obstructive male partners. A tutor involved in skills courses for
women in Scotland referred to the 'horrific incidence of harassment
of women students by their male partners, even in 1992.' A recent
survey of Access students in a higher education institution revealed
that one in three women had experienced domestic violence during
their time on the course and that many partnerships were under severe
strain as a result of their participation:

> From the start of the Access course staff were made aware of the
> intense pressure placed on women students to give up their studies.
> Women students shared many problems with their male counterparts:
> interrupted or inadequate schooling, lack of financial support, and a
> range of social and economic difficulties. For the women, though, there
> was always an added dimension: even today, those in heterosexual
> relationships continue to face concerted opposition from their male
> partners.
> This takes many forms, beginning with total non-co-operation in the
> home. Financial pressure is also exerted. In extreme cases, women
> were left with no money other than Child Benefit and so could not
> afford bus fares, paper, books or a cup of coffee. One woman who fled
> from her violent husband found herself homeless with a pre-school
> child whom the husband had taken away from her on the day of the
> final examination on the grounds that she could not provide a proper

*home. He offered custody if she would give up college immediately.
A miscellany of other techniques were employed. In some cases, the
wider family was recruited to reinforce a campaign of emotional
blackmail. Students' work was mocked by better educated partners (in
all social classes). What was amazing was that the women continued
the courses in spite of these obstacles and if they had to leave came
back again as soon as they could (Jarvis, 1992).*

A woman who had joined a women's singing class described to
the researcher how the husband of one participant used to bang on
the window and shout insults at the group. His wife eventually left
the class because of his opposition to her involvement. Opposition is
even stronger if a course entails a residential element, as a New
Horizons student found when she broached the subject of attending
a residential weekend: 'You would have thought I'd asked to fly to the
moon' (Gordon, 1992: 11). In her survey of short courses for women
at Northern College, Cole (1988) found women resorting to complex
subterfuges to make weekend courses appear less threatening to their
male partners.

Women who establish education centres or initiatives to help
themselves sometimes experience violent opposition. It is a common
experience for women's groups and centres that are not primarily
oriented towards reinforcing conventional female roles to attract hostility whatever their stated aim or function. One women's training
centre which attracts a large number of minority ethnic women is
routinely visited by men to ensure that it is a respectable and suitable
environment for their wives, daughters or sisters. In some cases, the
women's involvement is only tolerated because they are acquiring
work-related skills 'for the family rather than for themselves'.

In an interview conducted at another women's education centre,
the co-ordinator reported that her husband wanted to cite the centre
as 'co-respondent' in their subsequent divorce. Marital break-up is, of
course, a widespread phenomenon irrespective of whether women
return to education, and it could be argued that educational involvement merely brings existing tensions to a head. There appears none-
theless to be a strong link between marital strife and women's
attempts to do things for themselves which are not connected with
their family role. As one tutor observed: 'Where women are concerned, whether it's public or private, everything's done not to disrupt
the status quo of the family. Their own needs are incidental.'

Male opposition to women's self-development and educational
progress has been ascribed to the perceived threat these present to
male dominance in the relationship: 'An improvement in literacy
skills fundamentally affects the balance of power in a relationship and

threatens the dominance of the partner who is depended upon' (McCaffery, 1985: 65). It has also been ascribed to men's unwillingness to accommodate themselves to a situation in which their partner's domestic role becomes of secondary importance (Bridger, 1987: 69–70).

Not surprisingly, domestic problems are a frequent cause of drop-out among women, illustrating the extent to which cultural and domestic pressures often oblige them to neglect or submerge their own interests. Many, inevitably, opt to learn or train in areas which are non-threatening, culturally acceptable and therefore incur less opposition at home:

> *Women have been so conditioned by the primacy of their family roles that, caught in a sort of double-bind, they feel they must take the domestic subjects in which they already have knowledge and experience, and also because, if they are spending household money (their wages) on themselves, the would feel guilty if they wasted it on something seeming not so useful (Hughes and Kennedy, 1985: 148–9).*

The Constraints Presented by Sex Stereotyping

Theoretically, education should broaden girls' aspirations. In reality, education and training reflect gender divisions within the labour market which themselves reflect and maintain the cultural processes of sex-role socialisation that take place outside the workplace.

It is sometimes argued that girls and women perpetuate stereotyping by resisting efforts to encourage them into a wider range of subjects and occupational areas. This is a classic victim-blaming stance: 'women's under-achievement and ostensibly "free" choice to enter limited and stereotyped occupations is thus attributed to their own failure to capitalise on education provision' (Highet, 1986). Deere (1988) has observed a tendency among careers guidance professionals to assume that low ability rather than lack of encouragement and opportunity is the reason for many women's stereotyped aspirations and lack of qualifications. She argues that women's educational and occupational choices are influenced by a powerful combination of factors: sex-role socialisation, family background, economic structures, schooling, cultural values and personal motivation. Payne (1991) also attributes women's educational under-achievement to a number of interacting factors:

> *Gender socialisation and the expectation that women will bear the burden of all domestic responsibilities; divisions in the labour market*

21

which classify jobs as women's work or men's work; the identification
of technology with masculinity; indirect discrimination; the direct
protection of male interests, and sometimes unashamed prejudice
(Payne, 1991: 8).

Gender conditioning in schools

The power of the conditioning process should not be underestimated.
Ahuja (1992) refers to studies of British children which demonstrate
the processes that lead to sex stereotyping. A survey of five-year-olds,
for example, revealed that all the technical toys were being given to
the boys. There is little to offset the power of this early gender conditioning: girls are offered strikingly few untraditional role models, and
systems of education and training do little to alter gendered participation patterns and choices. A recent HMI report on how girls fare in
secondary schools found that depressingly little is done, particularly
in mixed schools, to alter stereotyped attitudes and expectations. The
report echoes the findings of earlier research in revealing significant
differences in teacher approaches to boys and girls; inadequate equal
opportunities measures; insufficient attention to the changing domestic and employment roles of the sexes in the school ethos, curricula
and teaching approaches; a paucity of women in senior positions and
on governing bodies; very little gender-based monitoring of achievement; and little positive action 'to raise the expectations and widen
the horizons of girls' (HMI, 1992). This supports Rendel's (1992) view
that: 'the covert discrimination of the hidden curriculum carries perhaps a stronger message undermining formal equality ... the differential treatment of girls and boys by teachers and the omission of women
from the content of the curriculum' (Rendel, 1992: 164). Riddell's
(1992) research in comprehensive schools in the mid-1980s indicated
that all but a small minority of teachers were either hostile or apathetic
towards the implementation of equal opportunities policies. The aspirations of girls, however, had undergone some change. Riddell
found that feminine culture was gradually shifting, with girls defining
their future lives in terms of work as well as domesticity. Boys' culture,
on the other hand, had not changed significantly, a situation mirrored
in studies from other parts of the English-speaking world. Riddell cites
a US study showing that boys still regard power over women in the
home as their natural right: 'a potentially explosive situation, where
male and female identities are on a collision path' (Riddell, 1992: 52).

HMI (1992) and a number of educational researchers have found
a widespread tendency in mixed schools to believe that girls enjoy
total equality simply by virtue of having equal access to the whole
school curriculum. However, Riddell has found that the ostensibly

free subject option choice system is unlikely to promote equality, since, in the absence of intervention or encouragement, pupils are bound to make sex-stereotyped choices based on cultural norms:

> *Most teachers failed to acknowledge any channelling process in the school and sex stereotyped subject choices were blamed on factors external to the school. The refusal to admit the school's part in reproducing social inequality was reflected in and supported by the option choice system, characterising pupils as free-floating individuals making choices in a social vacuum and accepting the future consequences of their actions (Riddell, 1992: 49).*

Equal opportunities researchers have made the point that far more needs to be done in schools to alter gender-based attitudes and expectations:

> *It isn't enough to play the numbers game, 'have we at least 50 girls in physics this year?' Even if this were the case, if girls in physics classes are still receiving negative messages about their worth, then little will have been achieved (Arshad, 1992: 61).*

> *Introducing IT into schools is not enough. They have to monitor how it is taught and what the take-up is and that means using gender-free examples in the classroom (Sulaiman, 1992).*

In other words, changes at a deeper level are required to counteract gender patterns that are the result of powerful conditioning and strong cultural messages about what are appropriate female activities, and this means significant changes in school culture and processes.

Stereotyping in post-compulsory education and training

The failure to tackle gender equality at a meaningful level in schools continues in the post-school system, in training and in mainstream further and higher education. Although the number of female students in further and higher education has grown rapidly, government figures show that male students are distributed across a far wider range of subjects than females, who are clustered into business and administrative studies, creative arts and design, languages and social sciences (DES Statistical Bulletins 1991 and 1992; EOC, 1990 and 1991). According to UCCA statistics, women obtain almost half of all first degrees in the human sciences, but only 12 per cent of degrees in computer studies and 15 per cent of degrees in physics. While there have been attempts to encourage girls and women to enter areas where they under-achieve and in which they are massively under-represented, the situation has in some respects worsened rather than improved. For example, the proportion of women working in information technology has fallen to 22 per cent and is still dropping (Sulaiman, 1992). As in schools, the solution to this may not be a question of simply trying to attract more women, but, as Arshad (1992) suggests, changing assumptions and 'rethinking society's attitudes to women in an increasingly technical age'.

Sex stereotyping persists within the training sector. National training programmes such as the Youth Training and Employment Training schemes, for example, mirror the gender-segregation and inequalities to be found in the labour market. Few concessions are apparently made to equal opportunities on the schemes and little attempt is made to raise girls' and women's aspirations. An investigation of the Northern Ireland Youth Training Programme found: 'no evidence whatsoever of gender equality in the programme' (quoted in McGivney, 1990b: 25).

Superficial measures to attract women into non-traditional fields have made little impact on their overall position. Brine (1992a), for example, argues that the way European Social Funding has been used in this country – i.e. mainly for training unemployed women in areas where they are under-represented – has actually reinforced labour market inequalities:

> Mainly working-class unemployed women have been 'encouraged' out of training for advancement in traditional job areas (for instance, textiles or clerical work), where they might have re-entered the labour market at a 'higher' position – with correspondingly higher pay and status and possible influence. Instead, training has been directed towards new jobs and jobs of under-representation, especially in the most obvious areas of 'traditional' under-representation.
> The effect ... has been that women are kept in positions of low status and low pay, with no power or control in areas of women's traditional work, marginalised in traditional male manual work, and excluded from the higher status, pay and understanding of new technology and electronics – training in this area being confined to the areas of low status, low pay, end-user skills (Brine, 1992a: 154, 160).

Even the sectors where women are the majority of learners have not fully succeeded in challenging gender-based attitudes and expectations. General adult and community education is sometimes criticised for the nature of the provision aimed at women, much of which is designed for female self-improvement 'with the result that the human being is stunted in favour of a restrictive, gendered one' (Cousin, 1990). Community education which is ostensibly student-centred and free of gender bias has also been criticised for treating women as deficient, as victims in need of remedial care, and for reinforcing their traditional roles:

When community educators set their prescriptive sights on women 'to identify and meet their needs' it is as mothers, homemakers, child-rearers and as social and economic dependents that they are principally defined. ... Limited and limiting definitions of women are being employed which are likely to restrict women to their conventional roles and to preserve the separation which habitually occurs between workplace and community activities (Thompson, 1981).

Women entering adult or community education are limited to the opportunities which are available and accessible, in every sense of the word. Bruce (1984) has argued that while community education ostensibly leaves people free to participate in the learning of their choice, it actually offers a limited number of options which reflect existing class and gender assumptions and reinforce the socialisation of women into accepting different and unequal societal roles from those of men:

The notion of individual choice is a red herring. I cannot accept that women 'choose' to have less education, more unskilled jobs and lower pay than men. As long as 'domesticity', sex-stereotyping and sexist knowledge-bases saturate educational systems, no individual women can be said to have 'choice'. The sexual and class divisions which persist in educational practice are not there as a 'natural' function of the differential talents and interests of individual human beings but because education exists in an ideological framework which justifies disadvantage in society and makes it seem reasonable and natural (Bruce, 1984: 1).

The Restricted Labour Market

It should also be stressed that in addition to being influenced by cultural norms and pressures, girls' and women's subject and occupational choices are often based on a realistic appraisal of the job opportunities available. Riddell's study in a comprehensive school in the south-west of England found that although girls had a heightened awareness of sexism and sex discrimination throughout society, they continued to choose traditional female subjects because of their perception of labour market realities:

Most [of a group of working-class girls] had little enthusiasm for secretarial work, expecting it to be boring and poorly paid. Their choice was strongly influenced by the local labour market: office work was one of the few areas likely to offer employment. Even though they thought that girls should have the chance to be mechanics if they wanted to, it did not strike them as a realistic possibility (Riddell, 1992: 47–8).

Thus the operations of a restricted and restrictive labour market play a powerful role in shaping female subject and occupational choices. This can be seen clearly in the case of certain groups of women. Black women, for example, tend to be concentrated in stereotypically 'female' jobs such as nursing, office work and social work and in low-skilled, low-paid service jobs such as cleaning or kitchen work, and semi-skilled jobs in manufacturing industry. This is not through any lack of talent or aspiration. A study of young Caribbean and African girls has found that they have both high aspirations and the freedom to pursue a full-time career. However, their occupational choices are not based on their abilities and preferences but are influenced by 'overwhelming institutional limitations and the severe economic constraints of a racially determined labour market' (Mirza, 1992). Women who have been out of the labour market for some time are unlikely to gravitate towards non-traditional areas when they seek to return. This is not just the result of the socialisation process which 'saps the aspirational energies of women once they become housewives' (Deere, 1988: 92); it again represents a realistic assessment of the state of the labour market. Hence Payne (1991) found it no coincidence that nearly all the women who went into computing after completing a Training Opportunities Programme were young, with a good educational background and had not yet started a family:

The lack of family ties may well have encouraged an adventurous spirit, but it also made it easier for them to envisage embarking on careers where full-time work is the norm and few concessions are made to family commitments ... Women in their 20s and early 30s are often too busy raising their families to think about training in a new field. By the time they are ready to plan their return to work, women who might have had an aptitude for computing may consider themselves or be considered by others too old (Payne, 1991: 60).

The exclusion of women from certain occupational areas

The evidence also suggests that there are strong forces operating to retain the gendered nature of different occupations and skills and their associated tools and machinery. Brine (1992a) argues that women are being steadily excluded from the development, control, knowledge and understanding of new technology and electronics. Linn (1990), has identified some of the processes which are used to exclude women from science- and technology-related work:

- gatekeeping and access barriers in the paid workplaces of scientific and technological production
- the development of a positivist and masculine character in the domains of scientific and technical knowledge
- the invisibility of women's contribution to technical and scientific innovation
- lack of recognition of women's technical skills
- failure to engage women in product production.

There is also evidence of male hostility to women entering areas they see as their domain. A report from Northern Ireland argues that young girls will opt only for training and employment which they see as open to them and where they will not face a hostile reception:

The occupational 'choices' girls make within a narrow range of female jobs represents a realistic assessment not only of what jobs they will be permitted access to but also whether they could survive and thrive within them. Studies which have documented the experiences of girls who have attempted to cross gender boundaries in youth training measures graphically illustrate that the prospect of surviving or thriving is unlikely ... They provide a picture of a largely hostile male environment in which girls feel isolated, harassed and excluded by fellow male trainees ... At a time when gender identity is all important, the contradictions surrounding the incompatibility of being 'female' in a male job by the undermining or discrediting of this identity by fellow male trainees, may quickly force girls to give up. Survival depends on the ability to implement complex coping strategies in order to survive ... It is clear that youth training measures contribute to this process by failing to provide girls with support and counselling to help them cope with a male environment (Equal Opportunities Commission, Northern Ireland, 1991: 58–60).

Thus a number of factors combine to keep women out of certain occupations. Moreover, if they do manage to enter new vocational areas, their gender is frequently used to downgrade the job. Brine (1992b), for example, refers to the:

phenomenon of shifting goalposts whereby women's achievement in formerly male areas becomes degraded feminisation, while high status shifts to new male-dominated fields. Instead of diminishing the sexual division of labour, women's educational achievements have merely redrawn the boundaries of horizontal and vertical segregation (Brine, 1992b: 160)

27

The division between paid and unpaid work

One of the ways in which women's disadvantaged position in the labour market is sustained is through the maintenance of an artificial division between unpaid and paid labour. Butler (1992) argues that ambivalent attitudes to women's domestic work have had a profoundly negative effect on their access to vocational qualifications and paid employment. She ascribes the resistance to recognising women's unpaid work skills to two factors: the male-dominated economic culture which has consistently excluded women from paid work 'except where there is an overriding benefit in allowing them into such employment' and to the perception of work in the home as a vocation undertaken for love, family approval and private satisfaction, i.e. as something entirely separate from and unrelated to work outside the home. This perception gives an excuse for treating women returning to the workforce as inexperienced or low skilled.

Butler argues that recognition of female skills would radically challenge the male economic power base and current systems such as pay and promotion structures based only on paid work experience. Sustaining the distinction between paid and unpaid work, therefore, has positive advantages for men in that it maintains their superior access to public and economic power structures. For women, it not only perpetuates their disadvantaged social and economic status, it also distorts their evaluation of the skills they have developed in child-rearing, household management and voluntary activities. Thus women tend to accept society's estimation of their unpaid work as unimportant and their skills as irrelevant to paid employment.

The Constraints Presented by Women's Own Feeling and Attitudes

Studies show that attitudes, perceptions and expectations shaped by class, race or gender have as powerful an impact on adult behavioural patterns as material circumstances. It has been found that negative feelings towards education (as something formal and class-based) and towards oneself (as being too old, not clever enough, etc.) are often the strongest and most resistant obstacles to participation in education and training (McGivney, 1990a).

Cultural attitudes to women inevitably influence women's perceptions of themselves, thus reinforcing and perpetuating their disadvantaged position. Women daily experience the paradox of living in a society which simultaneously promotes and extols the primacy of their family role and comprehensively penalises them for embracing it through such measures as: economic dependency, reduced pension rights, diminished opportunities in the labour market, niggardly maternity rights, limited protective legislation and inadequate social support such as day care for children and dependent adults:

> Domestic responsibilities are awarded no status and no reward. Although childcare may be rhetorically described as important, in reality many women find their years at home are isolated, unstimulating and lacking in any form of social recognition (Coats, 1992a: 258).

Societal under-valuing of women, as reflected in the nil value accorded their unpaid work in the home, their inferior position, pay and prospects in the labour market, the under-reported general and sexual violence girls and women in all social classes experience, and the sexist attitudes they encounter at all levels of society, inevitably produces the poor self-concept and low estimation of their own worth and abilities that is frequently commented on, sometimes with surprise (which in itself is surprising). According to a member of staff on the mobile LiverBus service visited during the project, many local women suffer from: 'a chronic lack of confidence arising from their position in life – their self-image is awful'.

Given the prevailing culture, it is not surprising that after years of home-management and child-rearing, many women believe that they are unskilled even if they possess degrees. A poor self-image frequently deters women from entering education or training, as they fear that they may not be able to meet the demands made upon them. It also reinforces a tendency to accept jobs that are in no way commensurate with their actual skills and capacities. Many of those who return to education initially sell themselves short. Virtually every report on women's courses observes that even the most highly educated of women describe themselves apologetically as 'only a housewife' and find it difficult to recognise and value the multiple skills they have developed in that role. A report on a project for women returners in Swansea echoes countless others in observing that, despite their personal diversity and range of skills and aptitudes, participants exhibited certain common tendencies:

- to undersell themselves
- to undervalue their experience
- to overlook the skills they had accumulated outside a work situation
- to aim lower than their ability levels (Morgan, 1992).

These traits are commonly observed in an educational context, as are the feelings of frustration and isolation that often bring women back to learning in the first place:

> *An awareness of feelings of boredom, discontentment with domestic duties, a feeling of being trapped within four walls. ... For some there were more intense feelings of loneliness and depression; for others an awareness of untapped talents and potential (Gordon, 1992: 8).*

The societal mores and attitudes to women that give rise to these feelings are rarely questioned and acted upon, just as the more frequent occurrence of depression in women than in men is often observed in medical circles but the links with women's position in society never explored.

Payne's (1991) analysis of TOPs trainees revealed that one of the main differences between male and female participants was that it had generally been much longer since the women had last held a job: 'Absences of 11 or 12 years were not uncommon, while some hadn't worked for over 20 years. Eight per cent had never worked at all compared with 2 per cent of men' (Payne, 1991: 27). It is difficult for those who have not experienced lengthy periods of domestic isolation to understand its negative psychological impact, although prolonged unemployment has begun to give many men an inkling of its effects.

Some ethnic minority women are isolated for different reasons. Lack of English is a huge problem for some, while others who are perfectly fluent in the language may still have difficulty with different registers and colloquialisms. The co-ordinator of a course for black women who has researched the area of black women and employment has found for both younger and older black women difficulties arise when nuances of meaning are lost or misinterpreted in interviews or selection procedures (Clarke, 1992). Living in an alien culture makes participation in activities outside the home acutely difficult for some ethnic minority women, especially those living in areas where racist attitudes are openly or violently expressed.

For all these reasons, a woman's first steps to do things for herself outside the family may be frightening, whatever the level of her qualifications and earlier career.

The Constraints Presented by Education and Training Structures and Provision

Surveys of women seeking to re-enter education or training reveal that many experience problems that stem from education and training policies and providing institutions. Many are deterred by:

- the absence or inaccessibility of information and guidance on opportunities
- lack of suitable part-time courses
- lack of affordable childcare
- fee levels
- geographical constraints
- travel time and costs (EOC, 1990; Oglesby, 1989; Chwarae Teg, 1992).

Other common 'institutional' barriers which have been identified by women both in Britain and across Europe are:

- programmes not sufficiently flexible to allow for women's domestic commitments
- insufficient training attached to traditional female occupations
- priority given to other categories of workers at time of recession and unemployment
- insufficient and inappropriate vocational guidance, special education and training measures for women
- an assumption that programmes organised for men will also do for women: 'The problems for women arise where it is not organisationally acknowledged that the women are subjected to the cultural social and domestic pressures of being women' (Oglesby, 1991: 137).

A former women's training officer claims that the problems listed above are experienced by women irrespective of age, race or social class. However, there are some aspects which particularly deter women with low educational attainment and low incomes. Here we should note the sheer difficulty, for many people, of finding a way into the education or training system at all. Negotiating the maze of bureaucratic procedures governing entry to education and training programmes is daunting to many women, particularly those in receipt of welfare benefits. This is not a problem confined to the UK. In her study of single parents in Norway, Gullichsen (1992) argues that the way public services are divided and administered makes great demands on claimants, who have to make sense of the sometimes conflicting criteria and procedures operated by two unconnected sectors – education and social services – and demonstrate sophisticated 'bureaucratic' competence in order to take advantage of the opportunities available. Gullichsen argues that before they can take up education or training benefit claimants need:

- to have identified and acknowledged a need or problem
- to possess the knowledge/information as to which rights and possibilities exist
- to know who/which body administers the particular benefit or measure
- to be able to overcome the purely practical and psychological barriers often associated with being a client (Gullichsen, 1992: 26).

A recent study of unemployed people's attitudes to and take-up of training indicates that confusion about benefit entitlement and fear of losing a small but stable income often override interest in participation (McGivney, 1992). Paradoxically, those most keen to participate in training – unwaged women who are not registered unemployed as they have not paid the required number of National Insurance contributions to be eligible for benefit – often experience difficulty gaining a place on national training schemes because of the stress on the long-term unemployed (Payne, 1991). Systematic budget cuts have also reduced the Employment Training programme's work with non-priority groups. In 1991, women composed only 31 per cent of trainees on the programme.

According to Payne's analysis (1991), the present policy on training, where employers and trainees are expected to pay the largest share of the costs, does not encourage women's participation. Women are less likely than men to have money to invest in their own training or to receive financial help towards training. By the end of 1990, only 30 per cent of Career Development Loans were made to women (Payne, 1991: 19) and studies show that female students in higher education borrow considerably less than male students (DFE Statistical Bulletin 7/92; *Education* 2 October 1992: 266). Payne (1991) suggests that women's caution towards applying for loans is understandable:

> *Women would be justified in putting their own financial position and that of their families at risk only if they could be sure of secure and well-paid employment afterwards. Their family commitments and the casualised nature of much of the employment open to them means that their expectations can never be as confident in this regard as men's (Payne, 1991: 152–3).*

The Curriculum

Lack of suitable part-time training courses has also been identified as a considerable problem for women. The continuing stress on full-time education and training courses in public funding priorities discriminates against adults who can attend only on a part-time basis, particularly women with domestic commitments.

Many research reports comment on the lack of training and qualifications available in women's traditional occupational areas. Some institutions offer training courses for women only in the most obvious areas of 'traditional' under-representation. In some cases this has been motivated by a desire to access European funding rather than a real commitment to equal opportunities.

A number of studies have identified a dearth of preparatory or introductory programmes for people who need to brush up their basic education skills before entering a mainstream education or training course:

Attempts to increase access to vocational education are being undermined by lack of a grounding in general cultural education on which to build specific training needs. Such an emphasis also militates against the spirit of equal opportunities where only a strictly vocational training programme is provided: often women are hindered from taking full opportunities of programmes because of the lack of requisite preparation or certain educational skills (Oglesby, 1991: 140).

This is particularly true of the Employment Training scheme, where the stress on outcomes often leads to the exclusion of those who are less educationally prepared (McGivney, 1992). It is also true of many education institutions which do not always provide introductory or Return to Learn programmes to help students prepare for more advanced, qualification-bearing courses and compensate for previous educational under-achievement. There is a widespread assumption, underpinned by education and training policy, that people return to education and training with well-defined goals. This is unhelpful to women who have been out of the labour market or a learning environment for many years and who have no clear idea about their future directions. Reports of Second Chance or Return to Learn courses invariably show that women tend to enrol without a clearly defined goal other than a general desire to change something in their lives and restore confidence (Gordon, 1992). Research into women 'returners' in Birmingham showed that very few initially had a specific course or job in mind: 'It was much more common for them to know what they didn't want' (Larden, 1988).

Lack of Support Services

Educational and vocational guidance

Women students who have been out of the workplace and learning environment for some years require help with making the right educational and training decisions. This is not always available in education institutions. In one visited during the project, only 'proper' (full-time) students had access to institutional guidance and counselling. Part-time students, the majority of them women, were denied this essential service, with the result that some, according to a weary Return to Study tutor, were taking courses at the wrong level or repeating levels they had already achieved.

Many reports on adults in education and training stress that the best learning outcomes are achieved when educational and vocational guidance are a continuous process rather than a brief, one-off encounter at the enrolment stage. In this respect, the Further Education Funding Council's emphasis on vocational guidance and counselling at the three key stages of learning – entry, on course and exit – is therefore very much to be welcomed.

Childcare

According to McCredie (1992), the wider access project at Rockingham College would not work without childcare, as over 40 per cent of the 110 women participants could not attend without that facility. However, most education and training centres and institutions provide at best a limited and inadequate childcare service: 'Colleges don't have the support or resources for proper childcare. They may have a crèche which is open for a certain length of time, but by the time a woman has left a child and picked her up, she may have missed 30 per cent of her class' (interviewee in a women's training scheme).

Women's need for this essential support is invariably regarded as 'a problem' by education and training providers. Cole (1988) describes the reaction to a request for a crèche at one college: 'The averted gaze and lowered eye count could hardly have been higher if we'd suggested subsidising the nursery with child pornography.'

Only special projects, schemes and centres for women, many with European or charitable trust funding, make childcare a priority. However, some women's education groups are now finding that institutions and LEAs are cutting provision because of the Children Act, which, according to a training provider interviewed during the project: 'is making it more and more difficult to provide childcare. Every time we want to mount a crèche in a different venue we need clearance and the registration costs are offputting. Under the Act, each Authority is required to set up guidelines, and interpretations vary slightly from one authority to another.'

In a letter to the researcher, a Director of Education in Yorkshire warned that, welcome as higher standards for childcare might be, education and training provision for women in his authority was at risk because of the legislation. The parts of the Act which caused him concern were:

- the need for full day care registration for groups where children are two-and-a-half years and under
- the need for full day care registration where groups meet for four hours or more per day even if there is a midday lunch break and where it is likely that individual children attend for less than four hours
- the costs incurred in meeting the physical standards required for full day care
- the costs incurred in meeting increased staffing
- the cost of full day care registration (£100 for each group).

There have been few or no budgetary arrangements to cover these costs and some groups were in jeopardy for the commencement of the academic year. Already we have seen community projects not recruit because of constraints on children under two-and-a-half years. We have recognised this problem in our guidelines by allowing up to two children under two-and-a-half years of age in sessional care groups.

Similar concerns were expressed in several areas visited for the project. Staff at two women's centres reported that they may not be able to continue childcare because of the spiralling costs, and, in one case, the regulation about providing extra toilets.

Unwelcoming Institutions

Many women are put off by the ethos and inflexibility of education institutions. The white male culture of much of the post-school education and training system can be daunting to women, particularly those from ethnic minority communities. Although there are wide differences between ethnic groups, common institutional barriers for black women have been identified as:

- an unwelcoming environment for black students
- few black staff to act as role models
- patronising and racist staff attitudes

- lack of support structures for black students, such as black counsellors
- no allowance made in teaching methods and materials for students for whom English is not a first language
- provision of a wholly western diet
- a European-centred curriculum
- lack of a black studies component in courses (Cole, 1988; McGivney, 1990b).

The institutional deterrents outlined above have frequently been identified in reports on women in post-compulsory education. They indicate that education and training providers are not yet doing enough to assist women's access and participation. To help women overcome many of the barriers they experience, providers need to examine all aspects of the service they offer in relation to women students, and to pay special attention to the three key stages – access, participation and progression: i.e. the point at which women move back into learning; the nature of the learning experiences and support they are offered; and the point at which they make the transition to other levels of education and training or employment.

Summary Points

- Despite the huge differences between women, many experience common barriers: practical and material constraints related to a woman's domestic and personal situation; psychological constraints such as lack of confidence; and structural and institutional constraints such as lack of suitable education and training courses.
- Domestic commitments and the career break create a major problem for women who wish to return to education, training or employment.
- Lack of finance and the dearth of good and affordable childcare are the most commonly cited practical obstacles to women's participation in education and training.
- Lack of transport is a substantial barrier for women in suburban and rural areas poorly provided with services and facilities.
- Isolation due to language problems and living in an alien culture is another considerable barrier.
- These practical and material barriers experienced by women stem from cultural attitudes, expectations and assumptions.
- Sex-role socialisation militates against girls' and women's participation in activities and interests perceived as being for males, and often limits their aspirations.
- Women experience constraints on their outside activities and physical mobility, and many experience opposition from male partners to their participation in education and training.
- Stereotyping in the labour market deters women from participating in a wider range of education and training fields.
- Stereotyped occupational choices are often based on a realistic appraisal of the opportunities available.
- Women's disadvantaged position in the labour market is supported by the maintenance of an artificial division between unpaid and paid work.
- Women's feelings, expectations and attitudes, arising from their position in society, are also powerful barriers to their participation in education and training.
- The range and nature of education and training opportunities and the ways in which they are designed, presented and delivered also raise barriers to women's participation.
- It is often assumed that adults return to education and training with clear learning objectives. However, women who have been out of the labour market or learning environment for many years have not usually defined clear learning or career goals.
- There are insufficient introductory programmes for women who

are not ready to participate in a formal education or training course.

- Education and training providers often lack the support services which would assist women's participation.
- Providers need to examine all aspects of the service they offer in relation to women students, and to support women at the three key stages: access, participation and progression.

SECTION 3

The Role of Informal 'Re-entry' or 'Threshold' Programmes in Assisting Women's Access, Participation and Progression

For all the reasons stated in Section 2, large numbers of women have neither the possibility nor the confidence to enter a formal education and training programme. The fear and nervousness many feel when returning to a learning situation after a long period at home should neither be discounted nor underestimated. It is a phenomenon that is familiar to tutors of courses for women and frequently mentioned in course reports. A report on an LEA 'Springboard for Women' course, for example, typically refers to participants' nervousness when they attended the first session and concludes that lack of confidence was probably the major reason why many who had made enquiries did not join the course (Pooley and Bowry, 1992).

Information received from education workers and tutors suggests that informal courses for women are attracting women who would like to train for a return to employment but who have avoided joining a formal training programme because they fear they will not be able to achieve the expected outcomes. A WEA tutor, for example, reported that some of the women on her courses had not joined TEC courses because of the conditions attached: 'They are intimidated by completion expectations and formal achievement goals. Many have fears around basic things such as being able to write, or do maths, and potential failure'.

Similar findings have been reported by people working in further education:

> It is impossible for someone with low self-esteem and uncertainty about their own ability to enrol on a traditional academic course ... Returning to study can be a terrifying experience because of the constant fear of inadequacy and failure (MacRae, 1989: 27, 29).

This problem can be alleviated by a sensitive recruitment process and many TEC courses for women have an extremely high response rate. However, many women with low educational attainment, little confidence and low self-esteem will need provision at an earlier stage to ease them back into learning. For this group, informal re-entry or preparatory programmes provide a non-threatening route back to learning and help women to develop the confidence and motivation to progress to higher levels of education or training. The evidence suggests that different types of course can perform this valuable 'threshold' role:

1. Some general adult education courses such as those provided by a Local Education Authority, the WEA or university extra-mural departments. Depending on their content, how they are taught, etc., these may or may not lead to transition to other levels of education. Many traditional adult education courses targeted at women do not aim to empower them or give them skills and are attended mainly by a middle-class and more affluent clientele.

2. Preparatory or introductory courses which have educational progression as the primary aim and which articulate with further or higher education, e.g. Access to Higher Education, Return to Learn or access courses provided by LEAs, colleges of further education, the WEA, etc.

3. New (or Wider) Opportunities for Women courses provided by LEAs, TECs, colleges, etc. to help women explore their potential and assist them in their educational, vocational or employment choices.

4. Pre-training courses (including women returner courses) provided by colleges, TECs, women's training projects, private providers, etc., designed to prepare individuals for specific work-related training and non-traditional skill areas; to re-establish basic skills; to raise aspirations; and to bridge the gap between home and paid work.

5. Informal community-based re-entry programmes, offered by LEAs, further education colleges, the WEA and other voluntary providers, aimed at groups who are generally under-represented in mainstream provision, and tailored to their specific interests and learning needs.

These types of course will appeal to different groups. As a broad generalisation, middle-class and more educated women often return to learning via general adult education and self-development courses, while those whose children are older and less dependent on them, and

Afro-Caribbean, African and Asian women, are often more concerned with developing work-related skills than with general self-develop-ment. These groups often prefer employment-oriented 'returner' or pre-training courses. Many women with young children, however, particularly those with low previous educational attainment and low incomes, will not consider formal education or training as a feasible or attainable option:

> Women around here have very little: no structures for them; no money for bus fares. Every aspect of their lives is disempowering. The whole area of further and higher education is shut to them (WEA women's tutor in a rural area).

These women will be more attracted to informal, locally-based activities – which they may not describe or recognise as educational – with other women in a similar situation to themselves.

The Value of Locally-Based Informal Learning Activities

The evidence from many informal community-based learning schemes is that the majority of their participants – women with no or few qualifications who have been out of paid employment for some years – would not previously have considered entering a formal education or training programme. However, as a result of their par-ticipation, a significant number develop the confidence and motiva-tion to enrol in a further education or training course and to seek qualifications. How does this process happen?

Mothers will often look beyond the family once the children have started going to nursery or school. As MacRae (1989) confirms, being involved in the community is often a woman's first step out from being with the family. The Women's Education project in Northern Ireland has found that for many women, the return to learning is a very gradual process: they start to meet other women through child-centred activities in nurseries, play groups, mother and toddler groups, primary schools or community centres with crèche facilities. Once a group is established, they may be encouraged to join a group activity (such as a discussion group) by a 'key' person (a nursery worker, head teacher or community worker) or they themselves may identify an issue or interest on which they want information and advice. These are often immediate concerns to do with child develop-ment, health and safety issues or lack of local amenities. Individuals with the necessary information may then be invited to speak to the group. This often initiates a series of discussion sessions which eventually lead some of the women to become involved in community education and subsequently more advanced and certificated programmes. According to the work in Belfast, the three conditions that enable this process to take place are the availability of local premises, childcare facilities and a 'key' person or worker on site: a person with local knowledge and contacts who is able to facilitate, advise, make suggestions, provide continuity and contact tutors and outside experts (McGivney, 1990b).

The importance of these factors can be demonstrated in any community education centre. What the process shows is that informal learning activities for women need not have educational or vocational progression as their primary purpose in order to lead to that outcome, and the majority of participants will certainly not have identified this as a goal. Preliminary findings from research into adult progression routes suggest that the desire for educational progression and accreditation often arises not before but during initial participation. A WEA survey, for example, has revealed that while students expressed a strong interest in progressing to other courses, over 60 per cent of respondents had initially enrolled on courses to build their confidence.

It cannot, of course, be claimed that all informal courses for women result in educational progression. There are a number of interacting factors which determine the development and outcomes of informal learning. A study of community education programmes for women in Glasgow has identified these as:

- socio-economic and cultural background
- interpersonal relationships (within the group)
- members' relationships with children
- the nature of the curriculum
- organisational structure and methods
- the role of the community education worker (Highet, 1986).

The information provided by the literature search and interviews conducted for this project suggests that courses and projects which motivate women to progress to other levels of education and training tend to have certain features and components in common. These include:

- women-only provision which responds to the education or training needs of specific groups of women
- conditions which enable attendance: accessible location; informal venues; provision of daytime courses within school hours; provi-

42

sion of fee concessions or other forms of financial support; some childcare facilities

- conditions which support participation: educational and vocational guidance; small group work; help with basic education, English language and study skills; tutorial or counselling support; a flexible, informal, non-patronising teaching approach; experienced and understanding women staff
- opportunities to share experience, to understand the link between individual experience and the wider social and cultural context and to look for ways to redress disadvantage
- components that encourage progression: confidence-building; assessment of existing skills, prior learning and experience; opportunities for accreditation; information on other education, training and employment opportunities; liaison and links with other sectors and institutions.

Responding to the Needs of Special Groups

The evidence cumulatively indicates that it is advisable at the re-entry stage to target specific groups of women. This is particularly important where there are wide cultural differences between groups of women. Different groups of women have different interests and needs and will more readily come together in groups from the same culture or similar circumstances. As Walters (1992) points out, when learners come from different positions of privilege or oppression, the sharing of experience is more likely to generate conflict than build solidarity. A black women's tutor interviewed for this project argued for some black women-only groups, pointing out that when there are only a few black participants, white women often take over and black women find it difficult to express some of their problems and shared experiences. The organiser of a New Opportunities course for black women also insists on the importance of recognising differences between women from Asian and African racial backgrounds: 'It is really quite unhelpful for providers to lump both together.'

Women-Only Programmes

The experience of learning alongside other women in a positive and supportive environment, exploring and celebrating similarities and differences not only enhances confidence and raises awareness but also changes lives (NIACE REPLAN, 1991).

Opinions on the value of single sex education are mixed. Deem's (1992) analysis of some forms of women-only education leads her to conclude that it probably achieves less in terms of overcoming women's inequality than is generally claimed, while Malcolm (1992) attributes the 'vulnerable state' of much women's education to:

a ... blind faith in the overriding importance of women-only provision outside mainstream education. The threat of a challenge to the prevailing academic culture has been siphoned off into a marginal area of activity, leaving the culture largely intact. As an added bonus, institutions have been able to use their women-only courses as evidence of a deep commitment to equal opportunities (Malcolm, 1992: 52).

Others argue that single sex provision does not reflect the real world; that it is not necessary for women's future success and actually perpetuates their marginalisation and segregation. Walker (1991) responds to these arguments by pointing out that the 'real world' of training, employment and the workplace is already strongly sex segregated and that much of education and training has been men-only for many years without being described as such. The Charities Aid Foundation (undated) takes a similarly robust stance: 'It is a curious view. If W.H. Smith took the same standpoint in selecting their magazines, presumably we would have only unisex publications.'

According to Walker (1991), women-only courses are beneficial only if they are part of a properly planned positive action strategy: a means to an end and not an end in themselves. Malcolm's (1992) view is that women-only courses and options are only likely to contribute to women's equality and real change in education if they become a normal and integral element of all mainstream provision.

Nobody claims that all women require single sex programmes. As Coats (1992b) observes, we cannot assume that all women need to make changes, either in themselves or in their circumstances, or that all experience the same circumstances and face the same disadvantages. There are, however, strong arguments for providing single sex re-entry programmes for groups of women such as the following, often overlapping, categories.

Women who have taken a long 'career break'

Many women who have left the labour market during the period of family formation return to activities outside the home via a women's group or organisation. According to Deem (1992), women's groups often represent the first non-threatening route to activities outside the home:

> *For women who are not engaged in full-time paid employment, women's groups represent a chance to escape from the privacy and isolation of the household even though the topics considered may sometimes still be oriented towards homemaking. Single sex education groups that women have organised themselves recognize, although not necessarily for the purposes of achieving radical change, that women share certain interests and hold a common position in society, particularly in the home, the family and community, hence building on women's 'lived experiences'. In order to achieve such education, women have had to struggle hard against ideologies of gender stereotyping and patterns of male dominance and power which try to confine women to the private sphere of the home and family, away from the public sphere of employment and formal political power (Deem, 1992: 286–7).*

Women with little confidence and a poor self-image

Wimbush's study (1988) showed that women at home rarely receive positive feedback from the 'chief beneficiaries of their labours' but that they receive greatest support and self-validation from other women. This is confirmed by Aird (1985), who describes the collective nurturing process that takes place when women become member of a women's studies group:

> *Dependency in a women's studies group is likely, initially, to be operating at an intense level because of the accumulation of unmet needs which women bring with them. The strategy by which these needs are met is one of mutual nurturing, for balancing the dependency in the group is a reservoir of caring skills built up among a group of women over a number of years of adult life. As the weeks go by and trust grows among the women, a network of responsive caring will be established which diffuses and meets individual needs. The process is internal to the group, and is not primarily focused on shaping women to external roles but on an equal recognition of need, ability, self-image and aspirations (Aird, 1988: 220–1).*

The opportunity to form bonds of mutual understanding, support and encouragement helps many women to overcome their low self-esteem and start planning for change:

> *Women's studies courses seek to reverse the deprivations which mothering of women by women inevitably entails in a society which does not give equal value to men's and women's aspirations and needs.*

> *The group objective is the growth of autonomy in individual members and the dynamic is one of support and commitment directed towards independence. The self-image which is generated is one of positive identification with the strengths and power of other women (Aird, 1988: 221).*

> *Often it is the group which gives them the support, the ready ear, the sharing of experience, the humour to try the changes. The incidence of group support among women learners is striking. They not only give support in shared experiences but they also co-operate in child-minding and study. Talking it over with friends who have common experience creates real confidence and a sense of individual worth. Study is less difficult if skills are shared (MacRae, 1989: 29).*

Women with few or no qualifications

For women with low educational attainment, negative school experiences and doubts about their learning ability, a women-only course or project is often the only available non-threatening route back into learning. At the Parents in Education course in Liverpool visited for this project, a woman admitted that she joined this rather than any other course because she knew the other mothers and would not be ashamed or intimidated: 'People wouldn't be against me here. They won't think I'm a dimbo.'

Some ethnic minority women

The cultural traditions of some ethnic minority groups make women-only groups a necessity. According to Asian tutors interviewed during the project, many Asian women require a single sex environment: they would not attend courses otherwise. East Leeds Women's Workshop attracts Muslim women students because: 'We are seen as safe and non-threatening and are therefore approved. Husbands come and vet first. For one Middle Eastern woman it is the only place she is allowed to go. Not many could come if it wasn't women-only'.

Women training in non-traditional skills

As pointed out in Section 2, women who wish to train in non-traditional, male-dominated skill and occupational areas often encounter unhelpful or hostile attitudes from male students and instructors. The Women's Technology Scheme in Liverpool initiated women-only National Certificate courses as a result of the realisation that former students were dropping out of mixed BTEC courses at local colleges:

Many of our women had felt enough confidence in their own ability to go on to National Certificate or Diploma courses at local FE colleges, but only two have ever gained any qualifications in Electronics. The reasons have nothing to do with lack of ability, but with inadequate childcare provision, lecturers who would rather teach a room full of 16-year-old 'lads' and the general inflexibility of monolithic education institutions. A women-only environment is crucial for support (interview with researcher).

For all these groups of women, single sex provision aids the re-entry process by providing the security and support women need when making the difficult transition between the 'private' world of home and the public world of education, training and paid employment: 'To feel secure is a necessary step for adults to start participating, enquiring and learning' (Pooley and Bowry, 1992: 4). Women's reluctance to return to learning in mixed learning groups has been frequently commented on in the literature of women's education.

Single sex provision provides a safe environment in which women can be free to express themselves. It has frequently been found that women returning to education are uncomfortable in mixed groups because of a male tendency to dominate discussion – a phenomenon described by Spender (1981) and commonly observed in educational circles:

When you start in education men try to get the better of you in class; they try to dominate and intimidate you. Women feel owt they say will make them look daft. After a while you can learn to think 'I'm as good as you', but not at the beginning (Co-ordinator of Castleford Women's Education Centre).

Observation of mixed adult education classes has repeatedly demonstrated that men normally dominate the speaking time unless firmly checked by the tutor. However, tutors only used to teaching mixed groups would often regard this as 'normal' and would not try to create a better balance (Bruce, 1984: 1).

The few male students dominated both the discussion and the tutor's attention. Some women never participated at all unless asked a direct question. The mixed group appeared to inhibit some women both from participating in the discussion and from talking about other topics with their friends (Deem, 1992: 301).

Thus single sex provision gives women an opportunity to express themselves more assertively:

Women-only groups create strong women who are used to being heard. Their assertiveness and confidence grows more effectively than that of women in mixed group classes (Jarvis, 1992).

To 'speak up' is often a new and exhilarating experience; to be assertive, to put your own view, a real victory. There are courses which clear the way; show the process. Women find these invaluable in rediscovering their often sunken identity (MacRae, 1989: 29).

Single sex provision gives women the rare opportunity to explore and analyse together the conditions of being female in this society. It validates women's personal experiences and puts them in a wider social and economic context (Pooley and Bowry, 1992: 4).

There are many indications that women achieve more in single sex learning groups. Jarvis (1992), for example, found that 12 out of 17 women studying in women-only Access courses obtained high pass marks, compared with four out of 29 learning in mixed groups. She concluded that opportunities for women to study 'without interference from men' would lead to improved completion rates and levels of achievement. All the women-only groups and projects visited for this project had an excellent record in giving women the confidence and motivation to progress into mixed education and training environments and employment, even though this may not have been the primary motive of many participants when they enrolled.

Recognising Women's Motives for Returning to Education and Training

Whereas women entering specific Access or training courses tend to have clear learning objectives, it is rare for women returning to learning via an informal threshold programme to have identified a specific learning goal. Gordon (1992) comments several times on the absence of clear-cut goals among a group of New Horizons students:

Most significant in motivations is the absence of any concrete 'goals' either short or long term. Perhaps when one first starts looking for new horizons, it is unlikely that they will be seen in such an obvious way (Gordon, 1992: 9).

Gordon points out that the assumption that adults have specific objectives when they return to learn creates difficulties for first-time returners, who sometimes feel pressurised into expressing goals which are impractical, unattainable or based on insufficient knowledge or experience. Underlying these, however, there are often less tangible motives which are closely related to a woman's situation but which may be difficult to define at an early stage:

- to build or restore confidence. This is one of the most commonly cited motives of women returning to learning although it is often identified only in retrospect
- to explore and develop one's own potential. Gordon's study echoes many others in showing that a large number of women re-enter learning to reassess their self-image and find out what they are capable of:

The term 'goals' would seem inappropriate as it implies an 'end' and this study suggests that it was the travelling, the moving on with confidence, that provided the new horizons and not the achievement of an end. Each road led to another with a sense of fulfilment at each stage but also with a new sense of 'self' and a will to continue with the journey (Gordon, 1992: 25–6).

- to meet others and escape from the isolation of the home
- to do something for oneself after long periods subordinating one's own needs and interests to those of others. Gordon (1992) remarks on the frequency with which the expression 'I wanted something for myself' cropped up in interviews
- to seek mental stimulation:

For those who had reached a good standard of education ... the general expectation was that it would provide the 'oil' and the 'kickstart' to re-activate a rusty brain. For those students [the course] was seen as a stepping-off point for further study and/or work opportunity (Gordon, 1992).

- to explore future possibilities:

The course was ... an opening of doors, a broadening of horizons, a finding out what had been missed in the past and what might be done in the future (Gordon, 1992: 23).

Research consistently reveals these as the dominant motives of women returning to learning. Larden's study (1988), for example, showed that their immediate needs were confidence-boosting, self-assessment, information on opportunities and encouragement and support to broaden their horizons as priorities, with obtaining a job or a place on a course as a longer-term aim:

One woman's articulated desire to stop thinking of herself as 'just a housewife' found an echo in every returner's heart and provided a starting point for our skills and self-assessment work with individuals and groups (Larden, 1988).

If we accept that women often return to uncertificated learning without a single, clearly formulated aim and that 'the process of re-orientation is not a simple one' (NIACE REPLAN, 1991: 40), then it is clear that re-entry courses for them should be exploratory, multi-exit and with a variety of purposes.

The Aims of Threshold Courses

Deere's (1988) research indicates the importance of including affective (behavioural) as well as cognitive objectives in Wider Opportunities for Women courses – and this is widely confirmed in the access literature and evidence from courses which have enabled women to move on in a variety of ways. These indicate that the most effective 'restarting' points for women are courses which confront their barriers, raise their aspirations, break down gender and racial stereotyping and encourage women to:

- regain faith in their own abilities
- develop self-confidence and self-esteem
- recognise and value their life experience and skills
- recognise and understand the experience and views of others
- gain or refurbish basic skills and study skills
- develop greater autonomy and control of their own lives
- develop a more positive attitude towards education and training
- seek information, advice and guidance about future possibilities in education, training, employment, voluntary opportunities and personal life
- develop the knowledge and skills to take the next step towards further education, training, employment or personal change.

Building confidence

If these aims are met, the crucial outcome, without which women may not move on in any significant sense, is the development of an enhanced perception of themselves both as worthwhile and talented individuals and as workers with valuable and potentially transferable skills. If education and training are to have successful outcomes for women, their negative self-image needs, as a priority, to be reversed. In many schemes this aim is subsumed within the all-embracing phrase 'building of confidence'.

The concept of confidence is so often used in relation to adult learners in general and women in particular that it has become a cliché, although one which women invariably use when talking about themselves. Growth of confidence is universally held by adult educationists to be an important, if not the most important outcome of educational participation. However, it is an elusive concept. As a state of mind rather than a tangible outcome, it is hard to measure using conventional 'performance indicators' such as examination results. Nevertheless, it has to be accepted as the first measure of the success of a re-entry programme for women, since virtually all who participate claim that greater self-confidence is their most significant gain. A recurring theme in interviews with New Horizons students, 10 years after their participation, was the change the course had made to their former poor self-image and low self-esteem: 'Looking back, the most obvious area spoken about was personal development and growth of confidence' (Gordon, 1990: 21).

Similarly, research into the outcomes of the former Training Opportunities Programme revealed that:

> *The benefit most often stressed by women though rarely mentioned by men was that training gave them confidence in themselves. This was the key factor, particularly for women whose daily lives had, for many years, been spent at home with children (Payne, 1991: 51).*

Developing awareness and understanding women's position

Many threshold courses also have the implicit aim to develop women's awareness and understanding of their position in society. In her study of Wider Opportunities for Women courses, Deere describes how they can help to reduce the sense of inadequacy felt by women who have experienced years of socialisation as housewives.

> *Although there is no formal input on the political implications of the position of the housewife in society, the women usually arrive at that awareness during the course. This is considered a crucial element in the process of returning to the public world and pursuing a worthwhile career. The aim is to raise awareness of the way in which socialisation has played a part in women's perception of themselves, in particular, in the way that the notion of 'housewife' has become negative, as typified in the almost universal remark made by the women at interview that they are 'only a housewife' ... They come to recognise that they have internalised and personalised the low status that our society affords housewives. Being able to relate personal experience to wider structural issues, reinforces the personal confidence that comes from group support and self-assessment (Deere, 1988: 56–7, 78).*

In some cases this aim is explicit. The WEA Women's Issues course offered within the Parent-School Partnership scheme in Liverpool, gives working-class women – many of them in a very difficult and disadvantaged social and economic position – an opportunity to explore their feelings about their situation in an organised way. According to the tutor, this process acts as a powerful stimulus to the women's subsequent progression to other interests:

> *The feeling I got was that they had all these feelings bubbling up but they needed someone to trigger them. The things we talked about were guaranteed to grab their interest. They've all had opinions about things and the course has given them a platform. The course addresses them as adults and their own situation. The main achievements are a kind of confident awareness and the ability to recognise the situation they're in. It sparks off all sorts of new interests (interview with researcher).*

Developing an awareness of other life roles

Courses which are effective in stimulating women to progress into training or employment encourage women to see themselves in more than one role and develop a view of themselves as workers, whether paid or unpaid. At the same time, they help women to deal with the guilt trap many are locked into when they become involved in areas unconnected with their domestic responsibilities. This is a particular problem with lone mothers, who, according to the study mentioned by Highet (1986), tend to define themselves solely in terms of their function as mothers. Recognition of this tendency has informed the design of a training course for unemployed single mothers in Bremen (Germany). The pre-training stage of this course focuses on psychological and social factors in order to encourage participants to view themselves in the role of paid workers as well as mothers. Participants are also encouraged to initiate changes in their domestic lives to enable children to receive and accept their mothers in the additional role of paid worker. This pre-training stage is viewed as essential to the development of women's commitment to the training programme and, subsequently, to employment (Von Kuchler, 1991).

Courses which fulfil the aim outlined above do far more than just help women to move on. Wimbush's study (1988) revealed the vital importance to women's physical and mental well-being of mental stimulation and greater autonomy to exert choices and decisions. A recurring theme in reports on women's re-entry courses is the extent to which they lead to personal and life changes.

Focus and Content

The content of a course is, therefore, the key to women's progression (in all senses of the word). Since different groups of women have differing needs, interests and aspirations at different stages of their lives, the content of threshold courses may be as varied as the women they are directed at. For example, those who wish to return to the labour force often request:

- updating of existing skills
- confidence-building and other personal skills
- training in new technology
- training to help with changes of occupation (Equal Opportunities Commission, 1990: 26).

There is generally a good response from women when courses of this type are offered and it may not occur to providers that introductory or preparatory training courses may also be required by the many other women who are not ready to start on a formal training programme. A CBI Gallup survey conducted in 1988 showed that many women felt they needed some initial training to bring their skills up to the necessary levels. Pre-training courses with components such as basic skills, introduction to new technology and modern workplace processes need to be provided for this group, who may not otherwise be able to take advantage of the training opportunities available.

Re-entry courses for women who have not yet identified specific educational or training objectives do not need to be narrowly academic or job-related. So long as they are free of gender bias, stimulate critical thought, widen horizons, encourage exploration of new opportunities, 'act as a vehicle for confidence-raising and offer entry to a process of personal change and growth' (Bruce, 1984: 1), they may have a wide range of foci. An analysis of the outcomes of participation in WEA courses suggests that there is often no close fit between curriculum content and learner outcomes. Learner progression comes from 'the confidence gained through a curricular process which makes use of the effective aspects of the learning situation' (Harkin, 1991). This is borne out by Deere's study, which revealed the value of Wider Opportunities courses that were related more to orientation and self-efficiency than to specific jobs 'with confidence-building and improved self-perception as important to women's progress as any vocational advice and guidance given' (Deere, 1988: 95).

The Women's Issues courses in Liverpool and the Women's Education Project in Belfast demonstrate that threshold courses which lead to progression can be explicitly related to a group's current situation and the issues affecting them. Health issues, for example, are a frequent starting point for women without qualifications. In a community education group in Glasgow: 'This theme was used not only as a way of improving knowledge, but also as a vehicle for facilitating discussion and developing an awareness of the discriminatory nature of society and how this affects women's lives' (Highet, 1986: 160).

Other threshold courses may focus on a particular skill. A tutor interviewed during the project referred to the role of short creative writing classes in building women's confidence and helping them to develop a critical understanding; to managage self-disclosure and to criticise and handle criticism. Attending such a course has been described by one participant as 'a crucial if agonising first step' that led to A-Level then university (Adams, 1991).

Traditional female courses can also sometimes stimulate progression, depending on the skills, tutors and course objectives. There are, however, fears that many traditional courses merely reinforce women's unpaid domestic role. Highet (1986), for example, argues that many women's courses in post-compulsory education treat women as the appendages of homes, husbands and children, and thus contribute both to sexual divisions in society and to female underachievement at all levels.

Many, if not the majority of traditional female adult education courses such as cookery, dress-making, keep fit – though developing useful skills – are not concerned with empowering women or moving them on in any significant sense. In some cases (for example, with groups of women who are particularly constrained by social custom and cultural tradition), such courses appear to act as a kind of 'containment', relieving women's isolation but in a way that is culturally acceptable by reinforcing their traditional position and role.

In some projects and institutions, however, tutors have used traditional female subjects to attract women back to education, to unlock their potential, develop their analytical skills and stimulate and motivate them to go further. Some mobile schemes for isolated women use domestic subjects as a means of enhancing basic education skills, while a project at Rockingham College uses them as a route to qualification:

> *Although women come with familiar aspirations, we encourage them to move into other qualification areas. Many of the skills taught in the project are stereotypical but we're using them as a base to raise skills in other areas and to try and get women to recognise their existing skills, to see in what other areas they might be applied. We also try to match the training we're offering to local labour market realities (McCredie, 1992).*

In such cases and when designed and taught in certain ways, traditional female subjects can act as a safe and non-threatening route back into learning, enabling women to re-establish confidence before entering an unfamiliar study or training area. According to a staff member on the LiverBus: 'women tend to look at traditional things first and the step back is often through them'. Moreover, as forcefully pointed out at Castleford Women's Centre, the disdain often expressed for 'women's' subjects such as flower-arranging and cake-icing is misplaced, since many women can make a living from these skills:

> The Government seem to think you only want the hard vocational things, computers, etc. To me the other things are just as important. We all have things like cakes and flowers at home. People want to buy them. Working on these things can also lead to jobs.

A similar point was made by an Asian tutor who argued that sewing is a very important, income-generating skill for Asian women who require traditional garments which are not manufactured in this country.

Course Components that Aid Progression

The testimony of many women suggests that re-entry or pre-training courses which fulfil the aims identified above frequently result in growth of self-confidence, personal development, changing perspectives and increasing clarity of objectives (Gordon, 1990). In order to help women capitalise on these positive changes, the curriculum needs also to encourage and support their possibilities of progression. The evidence from the literature search and interviews suggests the following course components which help women to move to employment or to other levels of education or training.

Core or basic skills

In a project conducted by the National Federation of Women's Institutes to accredit women's voluntary work skills, it was found that less academic students experienced difficulty with the basic writing and comprehension skills required to complete some of the independent tasks (Tiernan, 1992).

The importance of integrating general education skills in vocational education and training is beginning to be recognised both in this country and throughout Europe: 'The constant theme of feedback to [European] Commission offices from adult education agencies is the need to knit together the two [vocational and general education] approaches more' (Oglesby, 1991: 140).

Courses which target women whose first language is not English need also to offer help with English language skills as a priority.

Study skills

For women who have been out of a learning situation for many years, it often takes time to get into the habit of organised study. It is helpful therefore if preparatory courses provide built-in assistance with areas such as: locating and analysing evidence; making notes; reading critically; marshalling arguments and presenting them orally or in writing. Many of the courses and projects visited during this project had such features built into course design.

Educational and vocational guidance

An essential component of threshold courses which aim to prepare women for further education or training is continuing provision of up-to-date information and guidance on education, training and career options. According to Deere (1988), the advice offered should not be stereotyped but reflect a woman's actual and potential skills. She refers to the important role of guidance and personal action planning in Wider Opportunities courses:

> Women are learning about the labour market, career options, educational opportunities and are at the same time becoming more self-confident and increasingly perceptually aware. Combination of these leads to the formulation of plans representing realistic vocational choices. ... Action plans demonstrate the value of information, particularly when women are encouraged to find out about the local situation for themselves (Deere, 1988: 56–7, 91).

Planning for change

Through advice and guidance, threshold courses can help women identify desired changes in direction in areas such as education, training, employment or voluntary work. Elements such as assertiveness training and analysis of personal circumstances can also help women to recognise where personal changes may be necessary.

Job search and acquisition skills

Preparatory courses for women seeking to return to the labour market help the transition by incorporating such elements as help with analysing the local labour market, looking for vacancies, writing CVs, attending interviews and learning about the modern work place. A number of training courses for women visited during the project had also developed links with local employers and arranged visits to local firms and work placements.

Assertion and confidence-building need also to be a part of courses for women returners, since it is not always easy for women to make the transition from home to paid employment, particularly if they have been out of the labour market for a number of years.

Some groups, such as black women, experience particular difficulty in gaining access to jobs. In Thameside, a survey has been conducted of employer attitudes and expectations and black women's perceptions. The survey, which revealed the importance of developing social and communication skills, particularly in relation to white male members of staff, has informed the design of two New Opportunities (NOW) courses for black women. The NOW courses now incorporate sessions on communication skills and dealing with male colleagues, using methods such as role play (Clarke, 1992).

Assessment of prior experiential learning, experience and skills (APL or APEL)

Processes such as portfolio building and assessment of prior learning and experience are very valuable to women with no or limited paid work experience. These processes help women to identify their competences and skills in order to obtain qualifications, training or employment. The National Federation of Women's Institutes has piloted a course which identifies the skills women have developed in voluntary work in the community and leads to an RSA advanced diploma. The course has mainly recruited women from rural areas, all of whom, according to a survey conducted for this project, were anxious to have their long and wide experience of working for voluntary bodies accredited. The women, most of them middle-aged home-makers, had been involved for some years as workers and helpers in a wide range of voluntary organisations and many had also undertaken a number of general adult education courses. None, however, had any 'pieces of paper' recognising their experience, achievements and skills, which could be used to gain access to paid employment.

Butler (1991 and 1992) argues that the persisting view of women's unpaid work as a vocation implies that they have no competences or skills to transfer to paid employment other than areas such as caring occupations, where they are translated into low-paid work and low-level qualifications. However, work in the home often requires more complex skills than many areas of paid employment.

The unpaid worker in many ways already performs the required underpinning functions of paid work: autonomy, self-management, proactivity, team working, setting one's own standards, working to standard and taking responsibility for self-development. As an economic entity, the home demands the same type of functions as other economically active organisations (Butler, 1992: 98).

Butler cites the competence analysis project undertaken for Birmingham City Council Economic Development Department, which showed that the women were likely to have acquired up to half of the competences required for NVQ levels 1 and 2 for Administrative, Business and Commercial Awards just in carrying out normal household clerical tasks. They had also developed competences which corresponded with a range of other national management and supervisory standards.

The new occupational standards and vocational qualifications being developed by the Employment Department, Industry Lead Bodies, NCVQ and the awarding bodies recognise competences that have been developed in a range of settings. The NCVQ recommends that competence achieved in unpaid work should not be marginalised or seen by potential candidates as anything other than a standard progression route. In spite of this, and although there has been a national TEED-funded project to clarify and define the competences acquired in unpaid work in the home, unpaid workers are still far less likely to achieve credit for their experience and skills than those who have been in paid employment. There has been no guidance or directions from government to Lead Bodies on incorporating unpaid work into standards, and there is still, according to Butler (1992), widespread ambivalence in vocational education, training and employment towards the worth and transferability of competence acquired in unpaid work. In mainstream training environments, for example, it has been found that there is little understanding of the notion of competences acquired in unpaid work, as a result of which fewer women than men are accredited for prior learning towards NVQs. A survey was conducted in four colleges as part of an WRFE Development project on APL for women in non-traditional curriculum areas such as electronics and engineering. This revealed some confusion about the process among staff. Relatively few students had undergone APL and most of those were male. The survey found that there was no formal assessment of prior skills and knowledge and that most candidates were still gaining access to qualification-based courses through interviews and existing qualifications (Baillie, 1992).

Existing work on APL has nevertheless demonstrated its value for women. A course run by Barnsley TEC allowed women to acquire a qualification in business administration in 20 weeks by including an assessment of the skills they had acquired in unpaid work at home, voluntary work and previous paid employment. According to Page (1992) one of the most striking benefits of this process was the dramatic changes in attitude and self-esteem observable in the women undergoing APL.

> *The women were very modest about their existing skills, and it was only when we started to ask specific questions that they realised just how much they had actually done. One woman was practically running a farm, doing all the paperwork and book-keeping (Page, 1992).*

Accreditation

Accreditation has the dual advantage of providing tangible evidence of achievement and opening up possibilities for the next learning step. Many re-entry or threshold courses undertaken by women are not accredited, and some women returning to learning might initially be intimidated by the prospect. However, in some areas visited, courses for women offered optional accreditation at levels 1 and 2 through an Open College Network. Information from these courses suggests that once women have become involved in a course and overcome their initial nervousness, the idea of gaining credit becomes an attractive option:

> *Many are ready for this as it gives them a chance to aim for other than the domestic role. This term 50 per cent of participants opted to do the certificate and, as the weeks progressed, they all started to ask what else they could do. All of them want to continue in education in some form or other (tutor of WEA Women's Issues course).*

Several people interviewed for the project stressed the need to upgrade women's skills by offering properly accredited courses in women's traditional study areas.

Some Essential Features of Re-entry or Threshold Learning Programmes for Women

The evidence cumulatively indicates that the most effective re-entry or threshold learning activities for women share features common to all good community education, namely:

- they are open to members of the target group and involve no entry requirements
- they are relevant to and take account of the lives and experiences of participants
- they are organised in a flexible way to fit in with women's family commitments
- they have an ethos of equality of value for all
- they involve small group teaching and supportive teaching methods.

Aspects of course organisation and delivery which require particular attention are discussed in the following sections.

Sensitive recruitment

The literature on educational access constantly stresses that the most effective way of targeting groups is through localised contacts with community groups and organisations, co-operation with other agencies and local research to determine needs and barriers. Project workers at Rockingham College report that their most successful recruitment methods are visits by outreach workers to established community groups and word of mouth.

Providers of re-entry or pre-training courses need to have some awareness of cultural diversity and difference. In Thamesdown, a booklet has been produced by the Borough Community Development Division to assist this process. Entitled *All Thamesdown's People: Cultures and communities*, the booklet has sections devoted to a dozen or so different local communities who supplied details of their religious beliefs, traditions, diet, dress and annual festivals.

Tutors working with women also stress the importance of presenting and advertising courses in a sensitive, unpatronising and accessible manner – i.e. in a way that treats women as equals rather than as people who are in some way deficient; using a clear terminology which avoids jargon; using different community languages when targeted at different cultural groups.

Informal venues

The importance of providing an accessible and informal local venue for women returning to education has been recognised by many groups and projects offering routes back into learning. The National Federation of Women's Institutes offers in their residential learning centre, Denman College, 'a friendly, safe environment where our members can comfortably take that first step back into education' (Davies, 1991). Rockingham College has established a central and accessible venue, the Rowmarsh Room, to encourage people in non-participant groups to enrol in a range of courses leading to certification and progression possibilities. Rotunda Community College, based in a terraced house in the Vauxhall area of Liverpool, is open to the whole community and the atmosphere is friendly and relaxed. Ten women students of mixed ages, from a low income background and with no previous educational qualifications, were interviewed for the project. The women unanimously described the Rotunda as a unique resource and all mentioned the fact that it was a safe and non-threatening environment – 'like going into a home' – in which they were encouraged to develop their talents and potential. Some of the women had tried formal education institutions but had found them too formal and intimidating: 'We were treated like numbers. Here people treat you like a friend'. Interviewees mentioned former women students who had progressed to higher education but who still return on a regular basis to use the facilities and to help out as volunteer teachers.

Flexibility

According to people experienced in teaching women at the threshold stage, courses need to be both structured and sufficiently flexible to incorporate elements arising from experience, discussion and negotiation. Tutors working at this level stress that although forward planning is essential, some negotiation of content and methods is an important part of the learning process and hastens the building of self-esteem:

> For some, it is a revelation to have their suggestions listened to, discussed by their peers and then put into practice. They were surprised that they were thought enough of to count in the first place. Their previous experience had been more often being 'seen but not heard' and they had learnt to 'switch off' (MacRae, 1989: 27).

Negotiation is a key principle of many projects and centres which specialise in helping women return to learning. The Women's Education Project in Belfast, for example, always negotiates the content, timing, length and delivery of a course with the groups concerned. At the Women's Technology Scheme in Liverpool, staff conduct a continuing process of self-evaluation, responding to and incorporating student suggestions. At Castleford Women's Centre, the co-ordinator stressed the importance of asking women what they want: 'If you're starting a course for women don't assume you know what they want to do. We haven't put one course on which we thought of ourselves.'

This does not mean that the tutor is restricted to a facilitating role. It is essential in threshold courses for tutors to be actively committed to helping women to identify and implement their learning goals and to find the most appropriate ways in which these can be achieved.

Empathetic staff

Reports from successful informal learning schemes for women make clear the crucial importance of having people of the right calibre as organisers, tutors, outreach workers and guidance workers. A member of staff at a further education college, experienced in working with women at this level, maintains that the skills of the tutor are of paramount importance: 'threshold courses can't be given to just anybody.'

The co-ordinator of the Castleford Centre claimed that much of its success is due to the fact that it is run by people who love and are totally committed to what they are doing. The co-ordinator of the Rockingham College Widening Access project reported that choosing the right people to administer the recruitment, admission and induction of clients is one of the most important factors determining the success of any client-centred project.

In work with groups who are traditionally under-represented in education and training, it is important to have as outreach workers and tutors women from a similar social or ethnic background who are able to understand and empathise with participants' experience. The tutor of the Women's Issues course in Liverpool has found the fact that she shares many of the problems and experiences of participants extremely valuable in gaining the trust of women who 'always used to think of teachers as superior beings'.

Reports from projects targeted at working-class and black women indicate that women who enrol in formal education and training often encounter a marked lack of sensitivity and understanding from teachers and trainers, whose attitudes are often based on gender and race stereotypes. A tutor interviewed for the project also claimed that black women on mainstream courses often find white male tutors very patronising.

All the evidence indicates that tutors of threshold courses need to have empathy, listening skills and a wide knowledge of available opportunities and options for women. From her analysis of women's participation in TOPs courses, Payne concluded that: 'many would never regain the confidence to go back to work at all were it not for courses run by people who are sympathetic to their needs and who have the skill and experience to rebuild their faith in their own abilities' (Payne, 1991: 145–6).

Aird (1988: 220) refers to the complex relationship between tutor and students in women's studies courses: tutors are role models for students, providing an example of the possibility of action and self-direction. In another study Aird refers to the sensitivity of the tutor's role in handling the dependencies that women bring when joining a women's studies course, then gradually relinquishing their central role as students become 'more confident in the ability to think, learn, discuss, care about and support each other in the learning process' (Aird, 1985: 10).

Counselling Support

In a letter to the researcher, a former women's training officer writes:

From my days working principally with minority ethnic groups and women, I found that community-based schemes were not only needed to raise women's confidence to enable them to enter mainstream courses. Support networks were found to be equally essential.

It has almost become taboo to say that women returning to learning need support such as counselling, as some fear this will reinforce negative and patronising perceptions of them as people in need of therapy and remedial education. Thompson, for example, has criticised 'the lurch towards counselling and therapy models in women's education' (Thompson, 1989: 158). Nevertheless the need for sympathetic counselling is demonstrated by the fact that so many women return to education with two dominant feelings: a total lack in confidence in themselves and a need for positive change – however ill-defined – in their lives. Pulled in one direction by cultural and domestic pressures, undervalued, with their own interests and desires commonly submerged, many are unclear about the future direction they wish to take. Aird (1985) argues that courses for women need to engage with these feelings and include sensitive counselling in order to help women achieve new directions. She argues for non-directive individual and group counselling, not in any therapeutic sense but in order to 'validate the exploration of self and draw the group together as a support to the lives of others':

The decisions they make at the end of the course are closely related to the extent to which they have been able to clear space for themselves, both emotionally and practically, in the context of self-exploration that takes place during the course.
It is an important part of the tutor's role, particularly during the group counselling, that she is able to accept quite a burden of

dependence and to offer consistent, tactful and non-intrusive support
to women struggling excitedly, but sometimes fearfully, with the
recognition of their abilities and ambitions. The movement of the
course is from dependency to independency and this is manifest in all
aspects of the work (Aird, 1985: 20–1).

It should be recognised, too, that many women re-entering education are starting to do things for themselves after years of subjugat-
ing their own interests to those of the family and this can be a difficult
process:

It was the first time I'd gone off and done something by myself,
without children, without husband – a structure which is very
supportive but actually very destructive because you don't exist, don't
operate, as an individual – and you find it quite frightening to be
judged as an individual again (Gordon, 1992: 12).

Women returning to education need sensitive and empathetic
counselling not just to help them achieve positive change but also to
help them cope with the change process. Virtually all the course
reports read and tutors interviewed for this project referred to the
gradual and striking changes observable in women participating in
courses with the features mentioned earlier in this section. The increase in self-esteem and self-confidence that women experience is
one of the most important outcomes of re-entry courses for women,
since without it progression in any direction may not be possible.
However, such changes often involve adjustments in personal relationships and family roles. Many women, especially those encounter-
ing opposition from their partners, need support both from the group
and from individuals with appropriate experience and expertise, in
order to manage and cope with the personal issues that arise in their
lives at this time.

MacRae outlines the sometimes explosive impact of a woman's
changing self perceptions on her personal life:

A woman's new perception of herself and her directions often
challenge the old, easy, acceptable rubbing along whereby most
families live. Husbands and companions can find the 'new woman'
threatening; uncertainties escalate: 'What about us? What about
dinner?' The domestic situation deteriorates beyond what is acceptable
and sometimes there's simply nothing to be done but to leave. But
sometimes life at home is all you have and must be kept together
because it's very precious, the only haven in a hostile world. In this
web of relationships, the tensions and adjustments must be made
carefully. To assert can upset a precarious balance but some women
find the risk worth taking (MacRae, 1989: 29).

Adams (1991) describes what is now widely recognised to be a common process:

Academic success came at a very high price. As I had gained in confidence and knowledge, so I had grown away from my husband. Suddenly I was under the most enormous pressure, feeling acutely the disapproval and conflict of the immediate socio-domestic arena. The tension was unbearable and the situation untenable. I chose my education.

Support Structures

Other forms of support are required by women returning to education, particularly those who have been out of the workplace or educational environment for a considerable time, those with few or no qualifications, women training in non-traditional skills and some ethnic minority groups.

The kind of support needed varies. Some groups of ethnic minority women, for example, may need bi-lingual support, printed materials in their first language and courses which pay attention to their religious, cultural and dietary requirements. Good examples of the kind of support that can be offered are provided by East Leeds Women's Workshop, which offers one-to-one English tuition and has 10 days' 'flexible holiday' a year to allow for different religious festivals.

Some forms of practical support are required by large numbers of women, irrespective of race or class. Without them, they may not gain access to any kind of learning experience. Support in the form of day care facilities, childminding allowances or help with finding childcare (as now provided in some TECs) and help with eldercare are essential in helping many women rejoin education or training.

Threshold courses also need to recognise women's poverty and their inferior earning power in their fee structures. Where possible, providing bodies should provide fee concessions for women without personal or family means.

Other important areas of practical support which have already been mentioned are help with study skills and guidance services. These are important to all new learners whatever their sex.

All the features and components identified in this section contribute to women's successful participation in learning and their subsequent progression to other forms and levels of education and training. Many of these features characterise the case studies of good practice in the Appendix.

Help with managing the transition to formal education or training

Courses designed to encourage women's progression into mainstream education or training need to incorporate elements that will help students to manage the transition between the introductory and the next stages of learning. While most women-only threshold courses give women the vital confidence and motivation they need to proceed to formal education or training, they do not always equip women with the survival skills they need to face an unresponsive and sometimes hostile system. Many try and assist the transition process in practical ways, for instance by organising visits to providing institutions and inviting staff from them to speak to students. East Leeds Women's Workshop also offers a support service for former students who are free to return and discuss any problems they encounter.

Although women's threshold courses can provide advice and practical help with transition, they cannot, without a reciprocal effort by receiving institutions, affect or diminish some of the hurdles former students experience in moving to a formal education or training environment.

Summary Points

- Informal learning activities give many women the confidence and motivation to enrol in a further education or training course and to seek qualifications.
- The most effective re-entry schemes are those which target and respond to the needs of specific groups of women.
- Single sex provision provides a safe environment in which women returning to learning are free to express themselves and can explore and analyse together the conditions of being female in this society.
- Women have a range of motives in returning to education and training. To respond to these, re-entry courses need to be flexible and exploratory.
- The restoration of women's self-confidence and self-esteem should be the prime objective of courses which aim to help women progress.
- Informal learning activities for women need not have educational or vocational progression as their primary purpose in order to lead to that outcome.
- The focus and content of introductory courses may be as varied as the women they are directed at so long as they encourage critical thought, increase confidence and recognition of potential and raise aspirations.
- To be effective, re-entry or threshold learning programmes for women need to employ a range of approaches established in the best community education to target them, support their participation and assist their transition to employment or to other levels of education or training.

SECTION 4

Transition Between Threshold and Formal Education and Training Courses

After their initial return to learning, many women have a new perception of themselves and their capabilities. Although many subsequently move to higher level education or training, their progression is not always an immediate or continuous process. Gordon (1992) questions the assumption that adults trace a steady path through the education system. Her study of New Horizons students showed that students moved on at their own pace and when they judged the time was right. She also found that some experienced 'a big pull back to the family' before they moved into further education or training. A WEA tutor has also noticed that although a high proportion of New Opportunities students move on to other courses, there may be a hiatus or time lag before a further education or employment choice is made. Too rapid a follow-up after re-entry courses may therefore give a misleading picture of their actual outcomes.

The courses outlined in the Appendix actively assist and encourage women's progression into higher level education or training. The extent to which receiving education and training centres or institutions make efforts to accommodate women is a different matter altogether. The transition from informal to formal learning can be a difficult process for women. The elements of course content and delivery that encouraged their return to learning may be conspicuously lacking in the organisation and delivery of mainstream programmes, even when threshold courses for women are provided by the same institution. The information received suggests that women's courses in colleges often receive little in the way of support or recognition. For example, the staff of a black women's training course complained of being marginalised by the host institution: 'We could be offered a lot more in accommodation and support. We could be taken more seriously. We can't move forward as much as we'd like to. We've even lost our crèche and the students can't afford to use the main college one'. The general impression gained during the project was that women's courses such as this – though needed and providing excellent results – are often a tokenistic and neglected part of the work of large education institutions. Their importance in fulfilling the first educational needs of women – to gain sufficient confidence, self-knowledge and self-esteem to make clear decisions about their future directions – is rarely understood or appreciated: 'How do you translate women's feelings of progress into hard statistics which organisations will comprehend?' (Cole, 1988).

There was disturbing evidence from the courses and projects visited that many of their former students encounter little sympathy, help and support when they subsequently enter training or further or higher education. Follow-up of women who had participated in Wider Horizon days in Tyneside in 1991 showed that although 45 per cent had entered further education and training, many had experienced problems and setbacks (Focus On Women Consultancy, 1992). Others who had sought information and advice on appropriate education and training routes were defeated by the lack of information and interest they experienced in the further education sector: 'Some women were sent from one person to another, and the people they were trying to see eventually disappeared to a meeting. As a result, they left the college with nothing' (Co-ordinator, Focus on Women Consultancy).

The problems women experience in moving from an informal to a formal education or training environment arise largely because of the following factors: lack of information and guidance; lack of coherent education and training 'pathways'; domestic responsibilities and personal financial circumstances; and the fact that education and training providers are generally unresponsive to women's situations and their education/training needs.

Lack of Information and Guidance on Opportunities

This is so frequently identified as a barrier to progression that it deserves urgent attention. The following situation encountered during the project was typical of the progression problems cited in research reports and interviews. In one area visited, the higher education institution offers guidance only to its full-time students and the local LEA educational guidance unit had been closed down as a result of spending cuts. In consequence, part-time women learners attempting to move from a pre-training programme to higher level courses in the college had been trying to progress: 'without any help, support or advice whatsoever. They've been going round in circles because there's been no one to say you don't need to do that because you've already done it. They've ended up coming back to us' (Co-ordinator of women's training course).

Lack of Coherent Learning Routes

Interviewees working with women on other threshold programmes have found that some former students apply to retake the course because they cannot find an appropriate course to move to. In some cases, involvement in national training schemes had also led to a dead end: 'Women go to ET training and three months later they're back with us, starting from the beginning again. There's nothing for them' (Focus on Women Consultancy).

Information received during the project suggests that some education institutions which provide re-entry or pre-training courses for women make little attempt to provide coherent progression routes for participants. The courses are not always part of a curriculum framework with clear links between different courses and levels. Although this affects all mature students, it is symptomatic of a general failure to pay attention to women's overall education and training requirements. Whereas the threshold courses which have informed this project have identified women's needs and interests and gaps in provision: 'Colleges try to fit women into a structure that's already there and then make minor adjustments' (Women's Technology Scheme).

Lack of Support and Practical Assistance

Women who manage to locate an appropriate education or training course often encounter a range of practical obstacles which block their participation. From the information received, the two most common problems women face at the transition stage are the same ones they encounter at the re-entry stage: lack of childcare and finance. In both cases, there is evidence of a clear mismatch between threshold courses and formal education and training.

Most of the courses and projects for women contacted or visited during this project have made provision of or help with childcare a priority. Further education and training providers rarely demonstrate an equivalent concern. Follow-up of women who attended the Wider Horizons days in Tyneside revealed that lack of childcare presented the greatest barrier to their subsequent participation in further education or training (Focus on Women, 1992). When daycare is provided, it is usually for limited numbers of children, for limited periods of time and for a fee which many women find prohibitive: 'Although one of the local colleges has a nursery there is a fixed fee and our women can't afford it' (East Leeds Women's Workshop).

It is paradoxical that many of the access courses designed specifically to prepare women for an identified education or training programme offer childcare support, whereas the destination courses do not. MacRae (1989) quotes a successful Access student who could not enter university for this reason: 'They gave with one hand and took away with the other.'

As with childcare, many re-entry courses for women offer more financial support than the next stage of education or training. As a result, they may raise expectations which can be dashed when women try to move into mainstream classes: 'Most of our women are on low incomes and can't go on' (East Leeds Women's Workshop).

DeBell and Davies (1991) found that the difference between participation and non-participation in training was often just a matter of marginal costs. 'Unacceptably high numbers' of adults who had undertaken training were unable to pay for the examination fees which would have given them access to accreditation.

The current system of financial support for students in further and higher education puts women at a disadvantage. Many women can only participate in further education and training on a part-time basis but part-time courses do not qualify for grant support. In addition, a number of LEAs have cut the discretionary grants available as a consequence of spending constraints and the new funding regulations coming in under the Further and Higher Education Act. Moreover, if a woman wishes to go on to college or university and has not earned £12,000 in the three years before the start of the course, she will not receive the mature students' annual tax allowance (May, 1992). This discriminates against home-makers and low paid women workers. In addition, the student loan system may not help many women learners: in the current economic situation, women's prospects of finding well paid employment are not high and those aged 40-plus may have fears that they will not earn enough to repay the debt.

Jenkins (1992) has identified variations in LEA fee concessions as another obstacle to people wishing to move from community-based education to other education and training sectors. This diversity is being exacerbated by the restructuring of further education and public spending constraints on local authorities, both of which developments are leading to reductions in the numbers of people eligible for fee concessions and reduced access for those who are eligible. A college in the south of England, for example, is refusing to enrol students on any of its autumn courses unless they can pay the full fee. Applicants currently entitled to a concession – those receiving unemployment benefit or income support – now have to wait until just before the new term starts before they can sign up at the cheaper rate. The signs are that this particularly affects women applicants (Harding, 1992).

Entry Problems

Women who manage to overcome the twin obstacles of finance and childcare often encounter a further set of problems when they try to gain access to a higher level education or training course. Some providers employ entry tests and interviews rather than attempting to identify women's previous experience and skills. This can particularly deter women seeking to enter non-traditional areas. According to one report: 'If operated as an entrance test rather than an assessment of prior experience and learning, testing of mature students could erect another barrier against some mature entrants, particularly women' (Baillie, 1992: 13). However, as pointed out in the last section, there is still considerable resistance among employers and education and training providers to employing systems of entry which assess the skills and experience gained in unpaid work.

Unwelcoming Ambience

There is usually a considerable contrast between an informal local venue and formal education and training institutions. In some colleges and higher education institutions, the needs of a different student body are not yet sufficiently catered for and 'non-traditional' students, particularly if there are small numbers of them, often find they have to adapt to an inflexible, unwelcoming, sometimes hostile environment.

Many of our students progress to higher education – mainly the polytechnic as the university doesn't want mature working-class entry and is still resisting innovations like APL – but they still encounter inflexible attitudes even at the poly and tend to go in pairs (Women's Technology Scheme).

This is exacerbated by the paucity of women and black staff in senior teaching or managerial positions. Women often report that they encounter a lack of sensitivity from some male tutors and training instructors when they move into further education and training. Complaints about racial and gender stereotyping are common: 'Some colleges are very racist and sexist in their attitudes: they can present a very hostile environment for women' (East Leeds Women's Workshop).

Lack of Learning Support

Whereas many of the threshold projects and courses visited provide help with study skills, literacy and numeracy, often on a one-to-one or drop-in basis, further education and training providers do not always offer such support. This can create particular problems for ethnic minority and overseas students, for whom few allowances are made. Interviewees complained that teaching staff and training instructors often make misplaced assumptions about prior knowledge and fluency:

Many of our students do not have English as first language and this can present a huge problem when they go into further education. Here they get one-to-one tuition but this is not available in colleges (East Leeds Women's Workshop).

Measures to Assist Women at the Transition Stage

The picture regarding women's transition to the next stage of education or training appears therefore to be generally unsatisfactory. Informal re-entry courses for women give them the confidence and motivation to seek higher levels of education and training and many try to prepare them, psychologically and practically, to manage the transition. However, they cannot do the work of the receiving institution. Many women will not complete courses or achieve their highest potential if providers of training, further and higher education do not pay more attention both to the transition process and to the needs and experience of women students.

The evidence indicates that action in the following areas would not only help women to manage the crucial transition stage; it would also help education and training providers to improve their services and completion rates.

1. Improving inter-sectoral links and co-operation. Since it is clear that the gulf between informal and formal education is difficult to bridge not just for students but also for educationists, the first need is to establish or strengthen links and co-operation between sectors and institutions. In some areas this is happening through open college networks. Some institutions are collaborating with voluntary providers such as the WEA, recognising that the courses they provide can act as a bridge to mainstream programmes. Some funding bodies also recognise the value of voluntary bodies in assisting women's educational progression. In 1991, the Women's Education Project in Northern Ireland was funded by the Making Belfast Work programme to provide staged access routes from community-based education and training courses to further education, training and employment.

2. Improving the 'interface' operations of organisations or institutions, i.e. the points at which students first make contact. Priorities here would include:

*   offering an information and guidance service and always having staff available to respond to enquiries on courses and learning routes
*   taking account of women's perceptions of themselves in the way information and courses are presented. For example, many women may not think a course for unemployed people applies to them, as they do not identify themselves as unemployed
*   making entry requirements and progression routes clear and explicit
*   providing up-to-date advice on sources of financial assistance and the position of students who are benefit claimants
*   allowing people on restricted incomes to pay on a termly or otherwise staggered basis
*   supporting rather than marginalising any re-entry and pre-training courses provided in the institution and providing coherent progression routes for students taking them
*   reviewing selection processes in areas such as technical studies, engineering, etc. to remove gender bias
*   developing a system for assessing prior learning and experience

so that women who have developed skills in home management and unpaid voluntary work can access training at levels that accord with their abilities

- improving enrolment and admissions procedures
- offering mechanisms for induction and 'tasting' a range of courses across institutions, including non-traditional areas.

The admissions procedure has to fulfil certain 'external' requirements, e.g. completion of standard enrolment forms, etc. but at the same time be non-threatening to clients. Taster sessions provide a means by which students can attend without the formality of paperwork and begin to build friendships with staff and other clients. When formal documents have to be completed, it is approached in the most supportive and informal way possible (McCredie, 1992).

3. Improving the range and quality of education and training options available to women by:

- analysing the resourcing, accreditation and progression prospects of women's and men's traditional areas
- identifying where women are under-represented and taking measures to improve recruitment
- offering preparatory programmes for women wanting to enter non-traditional (e.g. technical) training areas but who lack the qualifications or experience for entry
- offering training and recognised certification in women's traditional occupations as well as in the areas where they are under-represented
- offering flexible learning approaches (distance learning, workshops, drop-in facilities, modularisation)
- offering exit routes that are as open-ended as possible. Women should not be lured onto courses under the false impression that they will automatically lead to employment.

4. Paying close attention to the quality of the learning experience and outcomes. Women's completion and success rates might be improved if education and training providers:

- provided mechanisms for curriculum support (study skills, maths, English, etc.)
- conducted continuous evaluation of progress and outcomes (in a wider sense than just examination results)
- provided student support mechanisms, particularly childcare or information about available alternatives
- provided a personal counselling service open to both full- and part-time students

- took steps to change the male-dominated ambience of institutions and some study or training areas.

The last of these factors is perhaps the most difficult to achieve as long as women are still under-represented in institutional management and while girls and women are still confined to such a limited number of curriculum and training areas.

The case studies in the Appendix detail some initiatives which have been effective in helping women to bridge the gap from re-entry programmes to more advanced education and training.

Summary Points

- Transition from an informal to a formal learning environment can be a difficult process for women.
- Although many informal re-entry courses actively encourage and assist women's progression into higher level education or training, some receiving education and training institutions make little reciprocal effort to welcome and accommodate women.
- Lack of information and guidance on education and training courses, levels and qualifications is a severe problem for many women seeking to take further courses.
- The two most common practical problems women face at the transition stage are the same as those experienced at the initial access stage: lack of childcare and finance.
- Some providers employ entry tests rather than attempting to identify women's previous experience and skills.
- In some education and training providing institutions, women have difficulty adapting to an environment and ambience geared to the needs of a younger and predominantly male clientele.
- Many women experience a lack of support and practical assistance when they move into a formal education or training environment.
- Completion rates and outcomes would be enhanced if providing bodies reviewed their practices and established a range of measures to support women when they move into a formal learning environment.

SECTION 5

Conclusions

The project has shown the extent to which the multiple barriers that deter women from participating in education and training and other activities outside the home stem from deep-rooted cultural attitudes and expectations underpinned by social and economic structures and policies. Since women's perceptions of themselves are largely shaped by society's attitudes to women, education needs to encourage a change in women's self-perceptions as a means of changing cultural attitudes to women. The project revealed the crucial importance of informal re-entry learning schemes which enable women to develop greater confidence and self-esteem and help them to take the first step back into education, training or employment.

The examples used to inform the project provide non-threatening routes back into education and training for women which are exploratory, which aim at increasing confidence and raising aspirations, and which support women's participation by providing childcare, financial assistance and guidance and counselling. It is a matter of grave concern, therefore, that projects with these features are fast disappearing. Although the need to provide introductory or preparatory programmes for women in education and training has been recognised in national reports from organisations such as the Equal Opportunities Commission, the Confederation of British Industry and the Trades Union Congress, all the evidence suggests that informal courses which facilitate women's passage back into education or training are now an endangered species.

Threats to Women's Re-entry Courses

A recent informal survey of current women-only courses suggests that they have an insecure future as a result of:

• budgetary and structural effects of the introduction of the Further and Higher Education Act 1992

- the transfer of funding and decisions from LEAs to colleges and LEA cuts
- greater stress on income generation
- changes in European Social Fund (ESF) criteria and the ESF budget shared by more courses
- the shift from developmental work to courses leading to accreditation and qualifications
- increased stress on short-term and sessional staff contracts
- the shortage of crèche places
- shortage of funding for crèches and spiralling costs of childcare
- outside finance (e.g. business sponsorship) hit by the recession
- low levels of grants, loans, etc. to women students
- low levels of political support for women's training (Coats, 1992c).

Coats' survey revealed a growing hostility to the continuation of women-only courses, which are widely viewed as exclusive, divisive, separatist, expensive and no longer needed.

The Impact of Policy and Funding Changes

The main threat to informal re-entry courses for women comes from policy and funding shifts and the changing culture of education and training that these reflect. Many of the courses and schemes read about or contacted for this project are experiencing increasing difficulties with obtaining finance. This is partly because of constraints on the public money available for training. Even Training and Enterprise Councils with a strong commitment to equal opportunities have had to reduce the scope of their activities because of the costs involved and in order to meet more urgent priorities.

Re-entry courses for women have also been affected by the increasing priority placed on tangible and quantifiable outcomes such as qualifications and employment-related skills. It is difficult to quantify the outcomes of courses which have as their primary function the rebuilding of confidence and self-esteem, the raising of expectations, and the recognition of women's own skills and potential. Thus some projects designed to ease women's return to learning are unable to satisfy the outcome-related criteria demanded by the Training and Enterprise Councils. During the project, a WEA tutor who had sought TEC support for women returners' courses found they were speaking a different language and that there was little understanding of

women's needs: 'It's very difficult. There's a constant battle of ideo-
logies'.

The Growing Culture Gap

The growing culture gap between different sectors and forms of adult
education will hinder the development or maintenance of education
and training routes for women. It is predicted that one of the effects
of college incorporation will be the weakening or severing of local
links between sectors that have been built up over the last decade. The
physical and financial separation of different types of courses for
adults, combined with the move towards outcome-related funding
means that the concerns, values and working methods of grassroots
educators are likely to move even further apart from those of policy-
makers and formal educators.

Structural Changes

Structural changes in the organisation and delivery of publicly-
funded adult education and training also threaten the existence of
informal women's courses. Women's courses which fit the funding
criteria of the Further Education Funding Councils may survive if they
can achieve certain designated aims. However, the diminishing requirement for colleges to conform to equal opportunities standards
and pressures on them to attract more students may oblige managers
to 'streamline' provision and concentrate on successful (popular)
courses for students who are cheaper to process. More expensive and
marginal areas of work with 'non-standard' students would consequently be dropped. There are signs that this is already happening. A
college lecturer who has been mounting successful short courses for
women returners for some years reported that although the courses
have a proven record of facilitating women's progression to full-time
college courses, they are now being cut because they do not generate
enough income (the women are unemployed) and because there is
funding for longer Access courses:

> I fought to keep these courses for 11 years but now that Incorporation
> is coming, no one wants to know about unemployed women at all. The
> university funds Access courses as feeders for them, but what will
> happen to women wanting routes to non-degree courses such as BTEC

*or GCSE? No one seems to care. Two-year Access courses – which
stress content not process and are too long and demanding for many
women – are crowding out the shorter preparatory and study skills
courses as there is funding for them (letter to researcher).*

Many LEA courses which fall outside the remit of the new Further
Education Funding Councils will have to pay for themselves. This
means that those which are aimed at affluent, white and professional
women may survive, but others aimed at socially and economically
disadvantaged women may not. Some women's centres and projects
receiving local authority support have already been affected by public
expenditure cuts. A women's training workshop, for example, has lost
its capacity to offer training allowances because of a freeze on the
council budget.

It is common for locally-based courses for women to lead a
precarious existence on short-term funding from special programmes
or charitable trusts. All of the innovative schemes described in a
REPLAN bulletin – *Learning Opportunities for Unwaged Women* (1987)
– started with 'funny money' (Cole, 1988) and most of them have
subsequently disappeared. The Women's Education Project, the only
model of its kind in Northern Ireland, has been struggling for years
on a mixture of short-term trust and special programme funding.
Other projects contacted have survived on funding from sources such
as Section 11 and City Challenge. However, these sources of funding
are under threat. In addition, several women's training projects receiving finance from the European Social Fund reported that it has now
become difficult to find the necessary matching funding. The matching funds requirement has been identified as a serious obstacle for
smaller grassroots women's projects and organisations seeking to
implement training initiatives (Northern Ireland Women's European
Platform, 1992). Workers with women also report that the criteria and
priorities of European funding programmes are subject to abrupt
changes: 'when the goalposts change, we have to conform to the new
criteria in order to survive'. Cole (1988) alerts us to the danger of
adapting courses to the needs of funders, but for many women's
courses this may be the only way of obtaining funding.

Nevertheless, European funding will continue to be an important
source of financial support for women's vocational courses and, now,
for guidance also. There is new NOW (New Opportunities for
Women) funding available and the Further Education Funding Council has announced that it will support accredited European Social
Fund courses. However, the overall amount of European funding
available for women's training is perhaps more limited than is generally believed. Brine (1992b) has analysed the European money avail-

able specifically for women and concludes that it is just under 0.4 per cent of the total funding allocation available: 'Of the cake women get the crumbs.'

The reliance on 'special' funding for women's re-entry courses, combined with the general failure to analyse women's experience and progress within education and training as a whole, precludes the achievement of full gender equality within education and training. This is analogous with the situation in overseas development, where outside funding to benefit women is used without any real commitment to furthering gender equality:

> Unless they (local agencies) are convinced of the validity, importance and priority of concerning themselves with gender analysis in a self-critical way, then no amount of 'pushing' will give rise to authentic – let alone effective – responses. Rather one ends up with a plethora of so-called women's projects (Eade, 1991: 306).

Workers in women's educational projects and centres attribute some of the difficulties they experience with raising money partly to the fact that their activities are for women. This is an endemic problem with all women's organisations. An analysis by the Charities Aid Foundation revealed that: 'there are no grant-making foundations specifically concerned with supporting charities and organisations oriented to the needs of women. Nor do there appear to be charities giving significant support by occasional grants and certainly not as a matter of policy'. Could this be, the author of the report asks rhetorically, 'because women in difficulties are still seen, unconsciously, as in some way disreputable?' (Charities Aid Foundation, 1991).

It is more likely due to two powerful facets of our culture: the hostility to women that lies only a fraction beneath the surface of acceptable social attitudes, and the persisting but unacknowledged urge to restrict women to the private domain. Both of these were strongly in evidence at the inception of the Castleford Women's Centre, an immensely successful education centre started by miners' wives: 'When we started they thought we were going to be a whore-house or a Lesbian Centre! They freaked out! After the miners' strike it were "get back to kitchen sink!"'

The Outcomes of Informal Learning

The effectiveness of the courses and projects visited or contacted for this project is not in doubt. They have a striking record in providing education and training opportunities for groups such as working-class, black and economically disadvantaged women who have been neglected by the formal system, and they are all successful in encouraging a large proportion of participants to progress to other levels of education and training or to employment. Castleford Women's Centre, for example, is now engaged in collaborative degree courses:

> *Who'd have thought I, a miner's wife, could be a teacher? Look at what we ordinary women have achieved: we've got four centres; a great variety of courses; 1,000 people coming a week – two-thirds for education and the rest for advice and information – and now we have 35 people doing a BA degree course in collaboration with Wakefield College (interview at Centre).*

This study has indicated that informal learning activities for women need not have educational or vocational progression as their main aim in order to lead to that outcome. So long as they are designed, presented and taught in ways that increase women's confidence and self-esteem, raise aspirations, stimulate awareness and critical thought and allow new opportunities to be explored, they will help women to progress in the ways most appropriate to them.

Transition Needs

The project found that while informal re-entry courses prepare women psychologically to move on by giving them confidence in their own abilities and raising their aspirations, there are still too many practical barriers erected by the current education and training system.

The findings suggest that improvements in financial support, childcare support and in the curriculum, ethos and approaches of education and training institutions would help women to manage the transition between informal and formal education and participate successfully in a more advanced education and training programme.

Financial support

DeBell (1992) points out that many of the (financial) regulations which affect adult learners stem from government policies which are not primarily concerned with education and training but with the control of public expenditure. The financial factors described in in previous sections – lack of assistance for part-time students, the complexities of the benefits system, reductions in discretionary grants and fee concessions – have a disproportionate impact on women's ability to participate. Many women have little money of their own to spend on education or training and there is substantial evidence that women with families do not use family money for their own training needs. The majority of women earn less than men and the uneven distribution of income within households means that unwaged married women may have little access to funds for their own purposes even if their partners are relatively high earners. This is not recognised in the rules governing eligibility for grants and benefits. Where LEA and college fee concessions are concerned, full-time home-makers are not regarded as unemployed, and, at the time of writing, the situation for people with little or no personal income is confusing and in a state of flux. As DeBell (1992) warns, full cost charging for many courses for adults may be one of the results of the Further and Higher Education Act and this will present a further barrier for women with limited disposable income and family responsibilities.

The Women's National Commission (1992) argues that women who do not receive financial help towards fees and other costs from local government or from husbands or partners are denied the opportunity to train or re-train. Their potential skills are therefore lost to the economy. The Commission calls for financial assistance towards a woman's training to be treated independently of any benefits her husband receives: 'Families should not suffer cuts in state benefits if women are awarded course fees since this discourages women from undertaking training' (Women's National Commission, 1992: 26).

The results of a vocational education and training voucher scheme initiated by Birmingham TEC demonstrate that large numbers of women will come forward when financial help towards training is offered.

Childcare support

If there are no childcare facilities to support day courses, many women will not gain access to even the first stages of education and training. Most of the re-entry schemes contacted during the project have made childcare a priority but some are now experiencing problems in complying with the provisions of the Children Act. The project also showed that lack of childcare support in further education and training is a major obstacle to women's educational and vocational progression. There has been no increase in public provision of care for young children to help the increasing numbers of women returning to full-time work: 'For the foreseeable future the disruption in a woman's working life caused by the birth of children is likely to remain a major factor in the under-use of their abilities' (Payne, 1991: 9).

MacRae makes a similar point:

If women are to go back into the workforce, initiatives must be taken by employers, government and educational institutions to provide the essential crèche. It is an issue management does not yet seem to take seriously. The result is lost potential (MacRae, 1989: 29).

There are, however, some hopeful signs. Gillian Shephard, when Secretary of State for Employment, made childcare the first priority of her Women's Issues Working Group. The 1992 Conservative Manifesto promised to introduce a new grant, via TECs, to help employers, voluntary groups and schools to set up after-school care and holiday arrangements. Some TECs have already made positive moves: Hertfordshire TEC and County Council, for example, have co-funded the appointment of a childcare co-ordinator to advise companies interested in establishing facilities for their employees and to help mothers make suitable arrangements (Women Returners' Network, 1992).

Institutional change

The evidence cumulatively indicates that women's education and training requirements are best met when providers:

- recognise and assess the experience and skills women have developed in their unpaid work so that they can start on courses and qualifications at appropriate levels
- offer educational and vocational guidance that is free from gender bias
- offer part-time and flexible programmes
- employ approaches which recognise and make allowance for the multiple barriers that impede women's participation in education and training.

Education and training providers need to adapt and change not only the courses they offer but also delivery methods, teaching approaches, support structures and general ethos to give women as well as men, black as well as white, equal opportunities to achieve. The project found that many women still experience difficulties when they move into a formal educational environment which is unwelcoming and unsupportive and where provision and teaching approaches reflect gender-based attitudes and expectations. The establishment of the conditions necessary to ease women's transition into formal education and training depends on whether providers genuinely intend to change structures and methods rather than just to attract women.

Although there have been some attempts by further and higher education institutions to improve access for women, relatively little has been done to ensure that the entire education and training experience is appropriate, responsive and supportive to women. This may be due, Cole (1988) suggests, to the ambivalence of some education providers in dealing with women: although they want to appear progressive and supportive of equal opportunities, any real moves to accommodate women are blocked because they create 'problems'. Similar observations can be found throughout the literature on women in education:

> *What nobody wants to face are the implications of having more women students – better playgroup provision, attempts to get more women staff, changes in course structure and content, changes in the behaviour of men in the college and so on. The close examination of assumptions, beliefs and material practices that would be needed cannot be contemplated (Hughes and Kennedy, 1985: 121).*

In many institutions, commitment to equal opportunities has been tokenistic and lukewarm. Action has been confined to some improvement of recruitment and access procedures for non-traditional learners, who are then expected to fit in with the existing system:

> *To go beyond matters of access to question social structures and institutions in a more profound way is extremely difficult. 'The problem' is still couched in terms of girls and women fitting into male career patterns and adopting male modes of behaviour, rather than questioning whether these need to change (Riddell, 1992: 52).*

According to many analysts, real equality within education and training will only be achieved when providers stop expecting women to fit in with the status quo and start looking for ways in which education and training services can be equally open and appropriate to both sexes. Few have any illusions that such changes will be easily achieved:

> *We should be clear that working for equal opportunities involves a serious challenge to power structures within education institutions which have traditionally worked in the interests of white middle-class males (Arshad, 1992: 61).*

> *If girls and women are to capture a greater slice of the educational 'cake', boys and men will have to give up their hold on the system – something they are unlikely to do without a struggle (Riddell, 1992: 48–9).*

Moreover, the impetus for change is low if education institutions (and employers) are not experiencing difficulties with recruitment. The literature suggests that in such a situation, positive changes for women only come about as a result of 'a strong push and struggle from below' (Cole, 1988) and the efforts of energetic and committed individuals.

It is generally conceded that to persuade education and training providers to adapt and change is no easy matter:

> *In trying to change we're working within structures and using rational approaches but really the problem is emotional and psychological. Things won't change if people don't want them to change. In the end, the most we can do for students is to provide access to what is available (interviewee in further education college).*

Education and training organisations and institutions reflect the values and mores of society in general. As Walters (1992) observes, the role they can play in changing women's overall position is limited. A combination of changes at political, social, economic and cultural levels are required to bring about any real improvement. Women's position will only change when there are significant changes in attitudes to women, their potential, their skills and their work. However, this is something that education and training providers can affect by recognising that women have potential and the right to the same life chances as men. This means acknowledging the disadvantages women face in a society that places supreme emphasis on employment status and competitiveness and making allowances for all the factors which affect their re-entry into education and progression within it: 'Rigid performance indicators based merely on cost, on statistical data or lists of simplistic competences are not sufficiently complex to cope with the many variables in women's lives' (NIACE REPLAN, 1991: 40).

The growing emphasis on 'family-friendly' strategies in training and employment is to be generally welcomed, even though it may have originated in the need to counter hostility to women-only measures. The findings of this project suggest that a more open, flexible and supportive system of education and training characterised by the features outlined in Sections 3 and 4 would be of great value not just to women but to all learners and trainees.

Summary Points

- Courses which facilitate women's passage back into education or training are an endangered species.
- Re-entry courses for women should not always be short-term. They need to be a secure and permanent part of education and training provision.
- There is a danger that the growing 'culture gap' between different sectors and forms of adult education will hinder the development or maintenance of education and training routes for women.
- Women's participation and progression within education and training would be greatly facilitated if there were financial support available for women in receipt of benefits, low waged or unemployed married women and part-time learners.
- Support for carers is essential to assist women's access, participation and progression. Women should not be penalised for bearing and bringing up the next generation and childcare and elder care should not be seen as a women's 'problem'.
- Real equality within education and training will only be achieved when providers stop expecting women to fit in with the status quo and start looking for ways in which education and training services can be equally open and appropriate to both sexes.
- Education and training providers need to adapt and change not only the courses they offer but also delivery methods, teaching approaches, support structures and general institutional ethos to give women as well as men, black as well as white, equal opportunities to achieve.
- If women are to gain parity of status and compete on an equal basis in education, training and the labour market, attitudes to them need to be confronted and changed.

REFERENCES

Adams, Christine (1991) 'Access through community education', *Adults Learning*, 3, 2, p 52.

Ahuja, A. (1992) 'You pilot, me nurse? No way', *Student Guardian*, September 29, p 22.

Aird, Eileen (1985) *From a Different Perspective: Change in women's education*, Breaking Our Silence series, WEA.

— (1988) 'Gender, education and change', in Punter, David (ed.) *Introduction to Contemporary Cultural Studies*, Longman, pp 212–22.

Arshad, Rowena (1992) 'The inter-connections of gender, class and ethnicity within educational contexts', in Brown, Sally and Riddell, Sheila (eds) *Class, Race and Gender in Schools: A new agenda for policy and practice in Scottish education*, Scottish Council for Research in Education, Minipaper No. 12, pp 60–4.

Baillie, Brigid (1992) *NVQ Audit in Non-Traditional Curriculum Areas for Women*, Lancashire Responsive College Unit.

Bates, S. (1992) 'Big rise in 16-year-olds staying on at school', *The Guardian*, 23 June, p 2.

Bateson, Beryl (1991) 'Community education and gender', unpublished BPhil dissertation, Westhill College.

Bridger, Sue (1987) *Women Learning: A consumer view of access provision*, Bradford Women's Employment Group.

Bridgewood, Ann (1992) *Women and Science and Technology: Strategies for practitioners*, Department of Employment.

Brine, Jackie (1992a) 'The European Social Fund and the vocational training of unemployed women: questions of gendering and re-gendering', *Gender and Education*, 4, 1/2, pp 149–62.

— (1992b) 'Fractured feminism: theory and practice', paper delivered to BERA annual conference, University of Stirling.

Brown, Sally and Riddell, Sheila (eds) *Class, Race and Gender in Schools: A new agenda for policy and practice in Scottish education*, Scottish Council for Research in Education, Minipaper No. 12, pp 44–53.

Bruce, A. (1984) *What is Women's Education?* Scottish Adult Basic Education Unit.

Butler, Linda (1991) 'Accrediting women's unpaid work and experience', *Adults Learning*, 2, 7, pp 198–9.

— (1992) 'Unpaid work in the home and accreditation', in Edwards, R., Siemenski, S. and Zeldin, D. (eds) *Learning through Life: Adult learners, education and training*, Routledge.

Chwarae Teg (Fair Play) Consortium (1992) *Expanding the Role of Women in the South Wales Workforce*, Chwarae Teg.

Centre for Information on Language Teaching and Research (1992) *Netword News*, CILT.

Charities Aid Foundation (1991) *Giving to Charities: A framework of disadvantage*, CAF.

Clarke, Dorothy (1992) *Results of a Survey into the Recruitment of Black and Asian Women in Swindon*, Workers' Educational Association, Women's Branch, Swindon.

Coats, Maggie (1992a) 'Women's education: the background', *Adults Learning*, 3, 10, pp 257–9.

— (1992b) 'The case for women-only provision', unpublished paper presented to the NAWO Women and Training Group.

— (1992c) 'Women-only education and training: the results of an informal survey'.

Cole, Ann *et al.* (1992) 'IT and gender: a guide to action,' paper delivered to BERA annual conference, University of Stirling.

Cole, Pam (1987) 'Do we need women-only courses?', *Working with Women*, NIACE REPLAN.

— (1988) 'Special educational provision: access to and experience of short courses for women at Northern College', unpublished MA dissertation, Postgraduate School of Studies in Applied Social Sciences, University of Bradford.

Courtney, Sean (1992) *Why Adults Learn: Towards a theory of participation in adult education*, Routledge.

Cousin, Glynis (1990) 'Women in liberal adult education', *Adults Learning*, 2, 2, pp 38–9.

Davies, Joan (1991) 'The voluntary sector: preserving diversity', talk given at NIACE conference on Adult Learning and the Bill, London, 27 November.

DeBell, Diane (1992) 'Paying for skills', *Adults Learning*, 4, 1, pp 7–9.

DeBell, Diane and Davies, Bryn (1991) *Paying for Skills: Financial barriers to access to vocational training for adults*, City College, Norwich.

Deem, Rosemary (1992) 'Popular education for women: a study of four organisations', in Edwards, R., Siemenski, S. and Zeldin, D. (eds) *Learning through Life: Adult learners, education and training*, Routledge.

Deere, Joyce (1988) 'Towards an understanding of women returners' vocational choices and strategies', unpublished MA dissertation, University of Loughborough.

Dekker, A. and Whitfield, R. (1989) *Completion Rates and other Performance Indicators in Educational Opportunities for Unwaged Adults*, NIACE REPLAN.

Department of Education and Science (1991) Statistical Bulletin, DES.
— (1992) Statistical Bulletin, DES.
Department of Employment (1990a) *The Skills Decade*.
— (1990b) *Labour Market and Skill Trends, 1991–92: Planning for a changing labour market*.
Eade, Deborah (1991) 'How far should we push in gender debates?', in Wallace, T. and March, C. (eds) *Changing Perceptions: Writings on gender and development*, Oxfam.
East Leeds Women's Workshop (1991) Annual Report.
Educational Broadcasting Council for the UK (1992) *An Analysis of the Second Chance Initiative Helpline*, BBC.
Equal Opportunities Commission (1990) *Training for Women: the future imperative. A discussion paper*, EOC.
— (1992) *Some Facts about Women*, EOC.
Equal Opportunities Commission (Northern Ireland) (1991) 'Girls and training: a research review', in *Sex Equality in the Youth Training Programme*, EOC (Northern Ireland).
Erskine, Sheena (1992) 'Gender issues: policy into practice', in Brown, Sally and Riddell, Sheila (eds) *Class, Race and Gender in Schools: A new agenda for policy and practice in Scottish education*, Scottish Council for Research in Education, Minipaper No. 12, pp 54–9.
Focus on Women Consultancy Group (1990) *Report of Progression Routes of Participants in Wider Horizon Days*, Focus on Women Consultancy Group.
— (1991) *Report of Progression Routes of Participants in Wider Horizon Days*, Focus on Women Consultancy Group.
Further Education Unit (undated) *Women's Link: Local innovation in adult education. Action research to determine the formal and informal learning needs of women in rural areas*, RP24(a), FEU.
Gordon, Margaret (1992) *New Horizons: Class of 80. Follow-up survey of 1979–80 student cohort*, University of Edinburgh Extra Mural Department.
Green, F. (1991) 'Sex discrimination in job-related training', *British Journal of Industrial Relations*, 29, pp 295–304.
Gullichsen, Anne (1992) 'Adult education for single parents (Norway)', paper submitted to the EBAE/DVV research workshop on Women and Vocational Training, Bonn, May.
Harding, L. (1992) 'New rule knock-back for college hopefuls', *Evening Argus*, 3 September, p 5.
Harkin, C. (1990–91) *Progression Routes*, WEA West Lancs and Cheshire District.
Hayes, E. (1992) 'The impact of feminism on adult education publications: an analysis of British and American journals', *International Journal of Lifelong Education*, 11, 2, pp 125–38.

Hedoux, Jacques (1981) 'Les non-publics de la formation collective', *Education Permanente*, 61, decembre, pp 89–105.

Her Majesty's Inspectorate (1992) *The Preparation of Girls for Adult and Working Life*, Department For Education.

Hester, Marianne and Florence, Penny (1992) 'Changes in adult education policy and the impact on client groups with specific reference to gender', in Miller, N. and West, L. (eds) *Changing Culture and Adult Learning: Papers from the SCUTREA Annual Conference, University of Kent, 1992*, pp 48–51.

Highet, Gillian (1986) 'Gender and education: a study of the ideology and practice of community-based women's education' in Westwood, S. and Thomas J.E. (eds) *Radical Agendas: The politics of adult education*, NIACE, 1991, pp 153–66.

Hughes, M. and Kennedy, M. (1985) *New Futures: Changing women's education*, Routledge and Kegan Paul.

Jarvis, C. (1992) 'Keeping them down: women and access provision', *Access and Community Education Studies*, 13, June, p 12.

Jenkins, Dianne (1992) *Bridging the Gap: Supporting adults into mainstream education*, final project report, Newport College of Further Education.

Larden, F. (1988) 'Just a housewife?', *Newscheck*, 5, 8, pp 15–16.

McCaffery, Juliet (1985), in Hughes, M. and Kennedy, M. (eds) *New Futures: Changing women's education*, Routledge and Kegan Paul.

McCorry, Mary (1988) *Women and the Need for Training*, Women's Education Project, Belfast.

McCredie, Tricia (1992) *The Widening of Access to Pre-vocational Education and Training and the Development of Progression Routes to Further Education and Training: Report of the Rockingham College Project*, Rockingham College.

McGivney, Veronica (1990a) *Education's for Other People: Access to education for non-participant adults*, NIACE.

— (1990b) *The Women's Education Project: An evaluation*, Women's Education Project, Belfast and NIACE REPLAN.

— (ed.) (1991) *Opening Colleges to Adult Learners*, NIACE.

— (1992) *Motivating Unemployed People to Undertake Education and Training: Some British and other European findings*, NIACE.

McIntosh, Sheila (1990) 'Human rights and free and fair competition: the significance of European education legislation for girls in the UK', *Gender and Education*, 2, 1, pp 63–79.

MacRae, J. (1989) 'More ladders than snakes', *REPLAN Review*, issue 5, October, Department of Education and Science.

Malcolm, Janice (1992) 'The culture of difference: women's education re-examined', in Miller, N. and West, L. (eds) *Changing Culture and*

Adult Learning: Papers from the SCUTREA Annual Conference, University of Kent, 1992, pp 52–5, SCUTREA.

March, C. (1991) 'Gender debates', in Wallace T. and March, C. (eds) *Changing Perceptions: Writings on gender and development*, Oxfam.

May, T. (1992) 'Higher education: The barriers go up. The increasing struggle facing mature students with dependents', *Everywoman*, July/August, p 39.

Mirza, H. Safia (1992) *Young, Female and Black*, Routledge.

Morgan, Jackie (1992) *A Bridge Between the Community and College: Report on the REPLAN Development Project*, Swansea College.

NIACE CYMRU (1990) *Outreach Work with Women*, NIACE CYMRU.

NIACE REPLAN (1991) *Women Learning: Ideas, approaches and practical support*, NIACE REPLAN.

Northern Ireland Women's European Platform (1992) *An Agenda for the Nineties: A briefing paper*, Belfast.

Oglesby, K.L. (1989) *Vocational Education for Women in Western Europe*, European Bureau of Adult Education.

— (1991) 'Women and education and training in Europe: issues for the 90s', *Studies in the Education of Adults*, 23, 2, pp 133–44.

Open College of South London and ILEA (1988) *Women Returners in Education: A conference report on the FHE Curriculum Development Project*, Open College of South London.

Page, Angela (1992) 'Credit where it's due', *Everywoman*, September, p 32.

Payne, Joan (1991) *Women, Training and the Skills Shortage: The case for public investment*, Policy Studies Institute.

Pooley, Bee and Bowry, Gill (1992) *Women Moving On: A bridging course between home, training and employment. A tutors' pack*, Berridge Centre, Stanley Road, Forest Fields, Nottingham.

Powell, Bob and Winkless, Carolyn (1992) *Adult Continuing Education Trends*, NIACE.

Rendel, Margherita (1992) 'European law: ending discrimination against girls in education', *Gender and Education*, 4, 1/2, pp 163–73.

Rendell, Ruth (1992) 'Issues facing rural women', *Rural Viewpoint*, 50, August.

Riddell, Sheila (1992) 'Gender and education: progressive and conservative forces in the balance', in Brown, Sally and Riddell, Sheila (eds) *Class, Race and Gender in Schools: A new agenda for policy and practice in Scottish education*, Scottish Council for Research in Education, Minipaper No. 12, pp 44–53.

Spender, Dale (1981) *Man-made Language*, Routledge and Kegan Paul.

Stott, Nigel and Pill, Roisin (1990) *Making Changes: A study of working-class mothers and the changes made in their health-related behaviour over five years*, University of Wales College of Medicine.

Sulaiman, S. (1992) 'Toys for the grown-up boys', *The Guardian*, June 2, p 16.

Thompson, Jane (1981) *The Educational Needs of Women in the Community*, Community Education Development Centre, Coventry.

— (1983) *Learning Liberation: Women's responses to men's education*, Croom Helm.

— (1989) *Learning the Hard Way*, Macmillan.

Tiernan, Kathy (1992) *RSA Advanced Diploma in the Organisation of Community Groups: Project report*, National Federation of Women's Institutes, Denman College.

Trades Union Congress (1989) *Skills 2000*, TUC.

Training Agency/REPLAN (1990) *Improving Access to Employment Training for Women. A regional partnership initiative in the North of England*, Training Agency.

von Kuchler, Felicitas (1991) 'Examples of professional training and retraining programmes for women in West Germany' in *Grassroots Education for Women in Europe*, European Bureau of Adult Education, pp 233–43.

Walker, L. (1991) 'The Glenand Project', a talk given on 28 March at Belfast Institute for Further and Higher Education.

Walters, Shirley (1992) *Training Gender-Sensitive and Feminist Adult Educators in South Africa: An emerging curriculum*, Centre for Adult Continuing Education, University of the Western Cape.

Whaley, Pat (1989) *Breakthrough Charter for Access: Quality provision for women in education and training*, North East Network for Women Learning, Northern Council for Further Education.

Wimbush, E. (1988) *Women, Leisure and Well-being: A study of the role and meaning of leisure in the lives of mothers with pre-school children. Research summary*, Health Promotion Research Trust, London.

Women in Consultancy Group (1991) *Evaluation of New Horizon Days held in Tyneside*.

— (1992) *Evaluation of New Horizon Days held in Tyneside*.

— (1992b) 'Women in view', *Focus on Women in Consultancy Group Newsletter*, 3, 4, Autumn.

Women Returners' Network *ReTurn*, Nos 1–7.

Women's National Commission (1992) *Women Returners' Employment Potential: An agenda for action*, Women's National Commission.

Woodley, Alan *et al.* (1987) *Choosing to Learn: Adults in education*, Open University Press.

APPENDIX

Courses and Initiatives Which Have Assisted Women's Access and Progression

The Women's Education Project, Belfast

The Women's Education Project (WEP) is financed by a mixture of charitable trusts, special grants and statutory funding. Its primary aim is to provide access to relevant learning activities for women with little or no post-school educational experience.

Since its inception in 1983, the project has responded to the learning requirements of women's groups in deprived working-class areas of Northern Ireland, across the sectarian divide.

The project provides free informal courses and tasters in response to interest and demand, with free childcare where needed. Workers visit women's groups when invited to do so and negotiate all aspects of courses with them. The courses requested have often been in women's health, assertiveness, basic education or creative writing, although more recently groups have asked for training in setting up and running their own organisations, including topics such as fund-raising and book-keeping. The project also organises and co-ordinates Women's Education Days at which information on the range of education and training opportunities is made available and taster courses are offered.

Where there are requests the project cannot meet, groups are put in contact with other providers.

The project has a proven record of attracting back to education many women who would not otherwise have considered formal education or training as a realistic or desirable option:

> It was the WEP which started us off on education. They did a series of taster courses and everyone really enjoyed themselves because it wasn't like school. Before, they were really scared of education. Now the majority of mothers here participate in courses (123 House).

> WEP courses opened up education to women who had all left school at 15 and 16. After this introduction, members went on to attend courses

provided by Rupert Stanley College, the WEA, and the Unemployment Centre (Roden Street group).

After taking WEP courses, the group embarked on a range of others – local history, literacy, Open University, courses using visiting tutors from the WEA and the local Further Education college. Some members went on to take GCSE English (Turf Lodge group).

During a recent evaluation of the project, many individual women maintained that, by starting them off on education, the project had been a major catalyst in their lives. All the women interviewed stated that the project's greatest gift to them was renewed confidence.

All the activities undertaken by the project are directed at increasing women's confidence and self-esteem. This objective is achieved through such means as:

- A democratic and participatory approach giving women control over their own learning: 'The power is with the women: they never take it away' (Divis group).
- Respect for women's views and experience: 'They give women an opportunity to talk and make them feel that what they have to contribute is important' (Ballybeen women's group).
- Use of women's own knowledge and experience in course content, teaching resources and learning methods.
- Sensitivity to and understanding of women's situation: 'They know the problems women have. They don't talk down to them or make them feel bad. They give women a feeling of self-worth' (Divis group). 'The women here felt they weren't equipped to approach outside agencies, but the work they did with WEP really enabled them' (Ballybeen group).
- Training in organisational skills to help women to organise and run their own voluntary groups.
- Training in tutor skills.

According to interviewees, the principal features which differentiate the WEP from formal providers are:

- the fact that the project goes to women rather than vice versa and mounts courses that respond to their interests and delivers them in ways that recognise their domestic commitments
- the fact that courses are free
- the personal and friendly style
- the ethos of support for women
- the project's flexibility and willingness to work with small numbers.

SOURCE: McGivney, V., *Evaluation of the Women's Education Project*, Women's Education Project Belfast and NIACE REPLAN, 1990.

East Leeds Women's Workshop

East Leeds Women's Workshop started in 1981 at a time when the clothing factories were closing down and the need for retraining was becoming urgent. The workshop was initiated in response to an identified need for women-only training in non-traditional skills. It is currently funded by the European Social Fund and Leeds City Council.

The Workshop offers one-year courses in carpentry and joinery, electronics and computing, with continuing support in maths, literacy and English for speakers of other languages. The computing and electronics courses lead to RSA and C&G qualifications, while the carpentry and joinery course is accredited by the Yorkshire and Humberside Association for Further and Higher Education. Students are also offered profiles or records of achievement which can lead to NVQs.

The courses are seen as a springboard into further education or employment, so student progression is actively assisted. There are optional job placements during the course; trainees are taken on visits to local colleges and employers; and there is an informal job club to help former students. In 1992, the workshop was seeking to appoint an Employment Development Worker specifically to contribute to this area of work.

Participants can enrol in the workshop at any time of the year. There are two fixed holiday periods: three weeks in August, two weeks at Christmas and 10 'flexible' days in addition to British public holidays to accommodate different religious festivals.

Enrolees are selected according to greatest need, with priority given to women from East Leeds and those who have difficulty in gaining access to mainstream education: women without qualifications, black minority ethnic women, women from overseas, women with dependent children.

Recruitment methods include outreach, leafletting, word-of-mouth and 'Have a Go' days.

During 1992, there were between 30 and 40 participants on courses at any given time. Their ages ranged from 25 to 60, with the majority in their twenties and thirties.

Most years, an average of 60 to 65 per cent of participants obtain employment or a further or higher education place. According to staff:

'The courses are usually a turning point. Few women don't change something in their lives as a result of them.'

Key features

The workshop has a number of features which account for its popularity with women and effectiveness in helping many progress:

- it is women-only and there is a strong ethos of support for women
- childcare expenses are paid and there is a childcare co-ordinator who helps find child-minders and after-school care
- courses are free; luncheon vouchers are offered and travel costs reimbursed
- the workshop recognises and respects the different cultural backgrounds of participants, e.g. by allowing 10 flexible days off for religious festivals
- women with a disability are helped, e.g there are trained signers to interpret for deaf participants
- courses are run on an individual basis
- overseas and ethnic minority participants are offered individual ESOL support
- students are actively supported in their transition to employment or further education (for example, through the informal job club; with help to find childcare so that women can go on to college).

SOURCE: Interviews with staff and Workshop Annual Reports.

The Women's Technology Scheme in Liverpool

The Women's Technology Scheme was established in 1983 to offer and improve vocational training and educational opportunities for women over 25, especially black women, women with no formal qualifications and single parents. The scheme is currently funded by Liverpool City Council and the European Social Fund. The curriculum has gradually expanded to include not only vocational training in electronics, micro-electronics and computing but also maths, science, communication skills, business and industry, the European dimension, introduction to teaching, women's studies and language training. It offers one-year, full-time BTEC and C&G courses, involving workshops, practical experience and theory, in electronics, micro-electronics and computing. Courses have built-in maths, general science, study skills, women's studies and guidance in career and further education opportunities. Participants have a week's full-time work experience with local organisations. The scheme has launched the first one-year BTEC National Certificate in Electronics for women and new courses in telematics and telecommunications involving transnational exchanges.

The scheme also offers a range of bridging courses, short courses and evening courses in technical and non-technical subjects, the latter accredited by Merseyside Open College Federation.

Key features

As well as the wide curriculum, the following features contribute to the scheme's effectiveness in attracting trainees and achieving excellent completetion, examination and progression outcomes:

- it is for women only which makes it easier for women embarking on non-traditional skills
- courses are developed in response to women's needs, and not vice versa
- students receive a weekly training allowance
- full-time childcare and holiday playschemes are available for the children of trainees, and during term time participants receive assistance with the costs of after-school care
- The long courses include support in study skills, general skills and guidance, and participants receive tutorial support
- management and staff, as well as trainees, reflect the composition of the local population
- management, staff and participants in the scheme all attend equal opportunities and anti-racist training sessions
- strong links have been forged with the business community in Merseyside, which assists student work placements and employment progression, as well as local economic regeneration
- employers connected with the scheme are expected to adhere to the project's equal opportunities policy.

Students' examination results are impressive, with many receiving distinctions. Progression rates to other forms of education, training and employment are high. However, 'the main reward of the programme is to see the level of confidence instilled in the women, who are empowered and motivated to achieve personal goals.'

SOURCE: Women's Technology Scheme literature and interviews with staff

Working with People: A part-time return to study course for black women at Goldsmiths' College

The 'Working With People' course was set up in 1986. It is targeted at black women with few or no qualifications, aged between 21 and 45, who are interested in working with people. The course offers a chance to return to study and to learn about and get practical experience in working with people, i.e. social work, community work, youth work and childcare work.

The course does not yet offer a professional qualification, although academic accreditation is being discussed and certification through the London Open College Federation is being negotiated. It helps students decide which type of work with people they are interested in, and acts as a 'first step' into further training or education.

The course costs £5.00. It is run for two terms and involves four days a week: two days on placement gaining practical experience in a community work, childcare or school setting, and two days in college. A block placement of eight weeks is built into the course. The course also involves a compulsory residential weekend.

Organisation

The course is located within the Department of Continuing and Community Education at Goldsmiths' College and as a whole is answerable to the management structure of the college. The project is responsible for its own administration, with back-up from the main college, mainly with typing and photocopying. All financial business is handled by the college. It is staffed by one full time co-ordinator/tutor, and one part-time tutor.

Premises

The project occupies the whole of the top floor of premises opposite the college, which consists in 1992 of one office, one classroom, a crèche (no longer running) and a spare room, used mainly for tutorials.

Aims

The primary aims of the course are:

To offer black women with no formal qualifications a 'return to study' opportunity with practical work experience in aspects of 'working with people' – i.e. community work, childcare, teaching, social work, etc. The course is seen as a 'first step' into further training/employment in this area of work.

To ensure that equal value is placed on the knowledge and experience of all women on the course and that this is used as a basis for the course content. In particular the experience and views of women who face discrimination on the grounds of race, class, sexuality or disability are reflected throughout the course content and teaching.

To provide support and assistance to students applying for further training and employment.

To challenge and find ways of dealing with racist or sexist attitudes within and outside the course.

Content

The areas covered by the course are:

- study and communication skills: essay writing, note-taking, speaking up in a group
- social studies, especially being aware of and dealing with racial and sexual discrimination
- introduction to social work, community and youth work and childcare work. Topics such as black and sexism awareness, child abuse, fostering and adoption, social work issues, mental health, women's health, probation, women in prison
- basic group work techniques
- basic counselling techniques
- help and advice on further training opportunities
- study skills are an integral part of the course.

Teaching and learning styles

Informal and formal styles of group working are incorporated into the course. A typical morning would consist of a formal presentation by the tutors of a topic, with students encouraged to take notes. The afternoon would offer a space for women to discuss and contribute to the topic from their own experiences. Sometimes visiting speakers are invited.

Progression

Nearly all course participants move on to social work courses, community and youth work courses and access courses. Some have taken up employment or voluntary work.

Key features

The key features of this course are:

* it is black women-only – which enables women to share common experiences and discuss issues such as racism, which many find difficult to raise in mixed groups
* it is very low cost
* it is preparatory and gives women the confidence and practical skills to progress to further training
* it offers valuable study and work experience, which aids progression to further training or employment.

Unfortunately another key feature – the crèche – was lost in 1992 as a result of financial considerations. However, staff are currently seeking greater financial support for childcare, travel expenses and general running costs.

As a basic education course we are well aware of the cuts being made to low profile courses, but it is hoped that our success rate over the past few years speaks for itself. The course has been of benefit to a lot of women who might not have 'returned to study' had they not done this course.

SOURCE: Maureen Patterson, Co-ordinator.

Women Moving On: A bridging course between home, training and employment in Nottingham

The course is currently funded by the Nottingham Task Force, and supported by the Berridge Centre, Forest Fields Neighbourhood Centre, Greenfields Day Nursery and Training Centre and Lynx Training.

The course started in 1988 and has run two or three times a year since then.

Course aims

* to enable women to make positive decisions about their futures
* to increase women's self-confidence
* to inform on education/training opportunities

- to develop skills to aid women to take the next step towards employment
- to provide ongoing support.

Target group

The course is intended for women who have had least educational opportunities in the past, and who live in inner city areas of Nottingham. This means that the support systems set up during the course can be continued afterwards. Women on the course often have young children and many are single parents. Their past employment experiences are of badly paid, unskilled work in factories, shops and bars. Participants on the course often have low levels of numeracy and/or literacy.

It is important to stress that the course is not a 'Woman Returners' course. It is designed for women who have never had secure, reasonably well paid employment and aims to give those women some degree of real choice about their futures.

Contacting participants

One-to-one contact is by far the most effective way of reaching the target group. Initial contact is made by the outreach worker through door-to-door knocking, local parent/toddler groups, schools and shops. Follow-up visits to the home are made by the outreach worker and a final visit is made by tutors where necessary. Leaflets and posters are used in recruiting women but only as a back-up to personal contacts.

The course lasts for 36 hours and operates during daytime working hours. A free crèche is provided. Visits to other establishments are made, for which free transport is provided.

Course content

The content of the course is based on the following themes, all of which assist participants' progression:

- transferable abilities: identifying skills women have gained through running a home and raising children and seeing how they can be used in a work setting
- confidence-building: women gain in confidence through mutual support whilst on the course. However, specific sessions on confidence-building are built into the course. These are designed to increase participants' self esteem
- job search skills: ways of gaining employment or getting onto a

course have changed over the last decade. This section of the course teaches women how to write a CV, apply for jobs or courses and improve their interview skills

- education/training opportunities: most participants go on to some sort of further training. Throughout the course, participants are informed of opportunities open to them. This is done both formally in the group and informally on a one-to-one basis as individuals begin to explore potential pathways. Visits are made to different training establishments throughout the course

- taster sessions on assertiveness and stress management: whether moving on to employment or training, many women need to increase their assertiveness and stress management skills in order to cope more effectively with changes in their lives.

As well as the course sessions, the tutors give individual attention to each participant and provide one-to-one career guidance and counselling on a more general level. After the course, tutors provide ongoing support to enable participants to achieve their goals.

Teaching style and approach

This course is primarily about women taking stock of their lives and realising the possibilities of doing something for themselves, so it is important that the teaching style and approach to the group reflect this process of empowerment. Attempts are made therefore to break down the barriers that create a 'them and us' situation. The group sets its own pace and defines, as much as is possible, its own agenda. This is vital for women who in the past have, on the whole, had negative experiences of school, where they have not felt in control.

There is an emphasis on group work rather than formal teaching, recognising that each participant has a valuable contribution to make. Group work is also used to enable women to feel secure, by recognising and validating each individual's past experience. Care is taken to give each participant sufficient attention and support.

Tutor skills include group work skills, teaching skills and counselling skills. The nature of the course dictates that tutors should also have knowledge of local training and educational opportunities and a knowledge of relevant agencies, e.g. helplines, DSS, crèche facilities.

SOURCE: From *Women Moving On: A tutor's pack* by Bea Pooley and Gill Bowry.

Rockingham College Project: The widening of access to pre-vocational education and training and the development of progression routes to further education and training

Rockingham College of Further Education has established a wide-ranging project, funded by the former Training Agency, on widening access to pre-vocational education and training and the development of progression routes to further education and employment. Aimed primarily at women returners, the unwaged and unemployed and people with disabilities, the project set out, among other objectives, to:

- provide a welcoming and non-threatening environment (a community-based centre, the Rawmarsh Room)
- support the development of an education and training framework consistent with the requirements of the NCVQ
- provide flexible access and clear progression routes (including the development of APL) from a community base to further education and employment.

Recruitment

Taster days and individual sessions were held throughout the year to facilitate recruitment and allow students to try out specific activities without commitment. Publicity and outreach work played a major role in attracting potential clients to taster sessions.

Eighty-seven per cent of clients at the Rawmarsh Room are women, mostly aged between 25 and 44. Over half of these are unwaged/unemployed and without qualifications. In March 1992, there were 110 women enrolees, 75 of them seeking qualifications to help them gain entrance to more advanced provision in further and higher education.

Key features

1. Providing a welcoming and non-threatening environment

The room which houses the project is part of the Youth and Community Block which stands on the Rawmarsh Comprehensive School campus. Both the school and youth service have served the local community for a number of years and have strong links with it.

The Rawmarsh Room has the advantage of physical accessibility, with a ground floor entrance and adjacent parking. Parking is on site and close to the room. Public transport is available to within a short distance of the room. All facilities required by room users are on the ground floor of the block.

It was decided at an early stage in the planning of the room to allow as much flexibility of layout as possible to accommodate the variety of subject and client needs.

The room was previously used as a workshop. It was equipped with benches and light equipment. Urban Programme funding was obtained to enable modification and refurbishment of the room, including:

- an effective heating system
- adequate power sockets
- a separate area for individual/small group guidance and tutorial sessions
- carpets, furnishings and essential fittings
- worktops for computers, sewing machines, typewriters.

The college provided essential equipment and materials such as computers, printers, typewriters, electronics equipment, a telephone and drink-making facilities.

2. Staffing

Funding allowed for one outreach worker, one clerical worker/receptionist, both full-time, and three specialist tutors who each gave one session a week. Rockingham College funded additional specialist and support staff, with the exception of an adult educational guidance tutor (provided by the Rotherham Unit).

The selection of appropriate staff was crucial to the success of the project. One of the major aims was to provide a welcoming, non-threatening atmosphere for reluctant or reticent clients, and the attitude of staff towards clients needed to reflect this aim. The staff also required other important qualities and skills:

- the ability to work independently of the main college
- an understanding of client needs
- an appreciation of prior learning and experience
- flexibility to deal with the roll on/off flexi-time requirements of clients
- a commitment to the project and its aims.

3. Supporting clients

To ensure that clients obtained maximum benefit and enjoyment from their studies, it was considered essential to provide suitable support mechanisms. These included:

- childcare support

- adult essential learning back-up
- educational guidance provision
- tutor support in general and specific subject areas
- friendly, empathetic staff available to listen to problems
- client-centred pace: clients are allowed to take as much time as they need to achieve the desired qualification.

Childcare support
Two qualified childcare workers supervised clients' children throughout all timetabled sessions. Funded by the College, as the Training Agency declined to fund it, this proved to be invaluable, allowing a number of mothers of young children to return to study.

Basic literacy/numeracy support
Tutors were carefully selected to assist basic skills development. Clients were able to receive help in basic skills through a subject specialist tutor; adult essential learning sessions with an ALBSU trainer; multi-craft workshop activities.

Adult educational guidance support
Staff from the Rotherham Adult Educational Guidance Unit were able to advise and guide clients on educational and vocational matters. The support given was based on client needs.

User group
With the assistance of the project outreach worker, the clients formed a 'User Group' which met regularly to discuss their experience of the provision, and make suggestions for its improvement and development. A representative of this group was invited to attend the advisory group serving the project, and to feed back the views of the group.

4. Supporting the development of an educational and training framework consistent with the requirements of the NCVQ and college-based provision
Six main programmes were available to clients attending the Raw-marsh Room:

- caring
- keyboarding/wordprocessing
- electronics
- identifying prior learning (women's APL group)
- adult essential learning (literacy/numeracy skills)
- multi-crafts

These were selected according to certain criteria:

- NVQ/VQ provision
- suitable resources availability
- allowing progression routes through NCVQ and other vocational provision.

The project framework encouraged student progression by credit accumulation and transfer and by the specification of equivalents. For example, GCSE Child Psychology and the St John Ambulance Public First Aid Certificate were respectively designated equivalent to two-thirds of the psychological aspects of child development unit and the First Aid component of the Health and Safety unit of the BTEC National Diploma in Nursery Nursing. Each gave exemption from their equivalent, and was accredited towards the BTEC qualification.

5. Developing progression routes
The first three programmes were chosen because they were part of the NCVQ framework. The others were selected to support learners. They all offered a variety of progression routes.

Educational advice and guidance on progression routes was provided throughout the project by workers from the Rotherham Adult Educational Guidance Unit, subject specialist staff working in the Rawmarsh Room and visiting speakers.

Clients were also offered: training on how to use computer and paper-based systems detailing progression routes; visits to other educational establishments such as Northern College; the acquisition of 'qualifications' towards a specific target.

However, a number of obstacles prevented smooth progression in caring and keyboarding/wordprocessing subjects. The major problem encountered by those studying 'Caring' was the amount of placement experience necessary to develop competence and the fact that the majority of care sector placements were not providing NVQ-oriented training at that time. Lack of keyboarding/wordprocessing equipment was the main barrier to progress for those wishing to acquire qualifications in these subjects. Clients were able to take RSA Stage One at the Room, but needed to attend a different establishment in order to fulfil the requirements of Stage Two. This highlighted the fact that the resources offered at a base must be carefully planned and sufficiently flexible to allow access to progression routes.

At the end of the year, the staff leading each programme were asked to map out the progression routes of their clients. The results revealed a variety of destinations, for example as a result of attending the caring sessions at the centre: two students joined the Playworkers Course at Rockingham; one student progressed to the BTEC National Nursery Nursing programme in September 1991; all the students in the group gained the St John's Ambulance Public First Aid Certificate. Employment routes included: teaching guitar at a private school; courier/holiday representative in Majorca; part-time jobs. Further/higher education routes included: full-time and 21-hour programmes at Rockingham and other colleges; open workshops at the Rawmarsh Room, Swinton and further education colleges; short courses at Northern College; the Mundella Programme at Sheffield University.

It is significant that most respondents preferred to continue working towards their specified goal within the community base, rather than transfer to other establishments.

SOURCE: Edited extracts from Project Executive Summary, Rockingham College, 1992.

REPLAN Development Project: Access to Further Education in Wales: A bridge between the community and college

This was a collaborative project between Swansea College and West Glamorgan Council for Voluntary Service in 1991. The aim of the project was to provide a bridge between the community and further education for women classified as 'hard to reach' who would not usually have the confidence, motivation or necessary skills to search out opportunities themselves. The targeted group had been identified as needing a particular kind of programme to enable them to move forward.

Recruitment

The programme made extensive use of the local networks of the Council for Voluntary Service (CVS) and the local networks around the Women's Centre. Posters and handbills were distributed to venues where they were likely to be seen by the intended client group, such as community centres, leisure centres, libraries, clubs, shops, etc. Eighteen women turned up to the first session and a core group of 10 followed the full course.

Delivery

The course was mounted at the Women's Resource Centre in Swansea High Street. A suite of rooms was rented, comprising one large learning space, a small counselling room, a large kitchen and a playroom for childcare. Although the centre was cold during bad weather, the style of the establishment was informal and fitted ideally with the aim of the project, i.e. the atmosphere and ambience were very different from those of a formal education establishment.

Two members of staff, both of whom were experienced in creating informal supportive environments, delivered the provision: one from Swansea College and one from the voluntary services sector. Such an environment was necessary to allow the women to work through the many barriers they faced in order to enter further education. The staff were able to facilitate development, to adopt a flexible approach to the needs of the group and to negotiate the learning. Experienced child-care staff were also employed to provide stimulating experiences of an educational nature. Up to five children used the playroom on any one occasion.

Delivery involved three-and-a-half designated hours every Monday morning over 10 sessions. There were some structured sessions, some informal sessions and some individual guidance and counselling. Coffee and conversation during the first half-hour contributed to the process of confidence-building.

The programme

The programme was loosely based on the Women Into Work module, for which CVS had received accreditation to the Open College through South West Wales Open College Federation and Access Consortium. The self-analysis pack involved looking at the women's strengths and weaknesses, an audit of their skills, interview techniques, and writing of a CV. These were the vehicles through which the women developed confidence, communication skills and assertiveness. They were also able to negotiate their own action plans. The whole experience was underpinned by a flexible approach to women's needs.

During the last two sessions, a minibus took the group to Swansea College. The group were shown around the college and given further ideas about possible progression routes. Some had previously identified specific areas of interest, and for these separate talks with relevant members of staff were organised. A particularly successful exercise involved linking the women with an existing group of students in Office Technology. Together they worked to produce good copies of the CVs which they had written earlier, with the college students wordprocessing the finished articles. At this stage, the aim of the project had been fulfilled; the women in the group had completed the transition and were ready to carry out their action plans.

Those women who wished to submit their course folders were

able to obtain a credit from the Open College. A moderator visited the course on the last day at the centre.

Progression

At the end of the course, all students had plans to continue and extend their studies. For example, two of the group were making enquiries regarding social care courses; at least one intended to update her skills in office technology, and one applied for work with voluntary organisations as the next stage of her personal and professional development.

The group decided that they would like some literacy and numeracy and some further assertiveness classes. It was therefore planned to use the Women's Centre as an outreach base for the college where these courses could be mounted. One of the group who undertook the Access course will be responsible for teaching this further provision. She qualified as a teacher some decades ago.

In the event the plans with the Women's Centre could not be implemented but as a result of links made with the ABE Co-ordinator, collaborative activities in the areas identified were initiated at the Open Learning Centre.

The women from the course continued to meet socially as an informal support group and all are progressing along their own individual routes.

SOURCE: Jackie Morgan, Swansea College, 1992.

Wider Horizon Days for Women

These one-day events in Tyneside are designed and developed by the Newcastle-based Focus on Women Consultancy with funding from Tyneside TEC. As they are geared towards helping women to return to education, training, employment or enterprise, the days are organised on a collaborative basis involving representatives from a wide range of education and training bodies. The days are particularly helpful to women who have defined a need to move on but who are not sure of the best direction for them. They:

- provide information on the choices available to participants and the kinds of agencies available to provide help and support during the returning process
- help participants to review their previous life experience both in the paid workplace and the home in order to identify existing

skills and areas of strength and to identify areas for future development

- help participants to embark upon the process of confidence-building
- help participants to prepare for the next step by developing awareness of the kinds of questions that need to be asked in order to maximise the help other agencies can offer.

The programme of the days involves:

- presentations to the whole group by 'role models' who give an account of their own routes back into education, training or employment
- small group sessions to help women evaluate their past experience, strengths and barriers to progress – using individual work booklets
- an information and advice fair – with stands for representatives of community education, further and higher education, careers services, employment services, the TEC and employers
- presentations by local education and training providers, including the local TEC
- small group sessions devoted to goal setting and action planning
- whole group review and feedback session. This session has shown that the role model presentations are particularly appreciated and has informed the sequence of sessions at subsequent events.

Participants are followed up three months after the events. This is a valuable way of evaluating how useful the days have been. For example, follow-up of 106 participants who had been involved in the 1990 events showed that:

- 33 per cent had entered education and training
- 26 per cent were still negotiating with and seeking advice from the organisations identified during the days
- 10 per cent had taken paid employment
- 6 per cent were actively seeking work
- 4 per cent were engaged in voluntary work
- 9 per cent had not yet initiated change as they were working on short-term contracts which had not yet come to an end
- 11 per cent had taken no action because of ill health or changed family circumstances.

Key features

- the days are free, with free crèche and lunch provided

- the group's views and perceptions of the programme are taken into account in the planning of subsequent events
- the small group sessions are valuable in boosting confidence and identifying strengths and existing skills:

  Most find it difficult initially to recognise existing skills and areas of strength but they grow in confidence during the small group discussions. Eventually a list of shared skills and strengths is generated, including organisational skills, communication skills, practical mechanical skills, skills in dealing with people, managing people, negotiating, etc.

- representatives of local education, training and employment agencies are brought together in one place and provide a great deal of information to which participants would not otherwise have easy access
- there is personal help and advice on goal setting and drawing up action plans.

SOURCE: Focus on Women Consultancy.